Boys from the Blackstuff

James Graham

T0027177

methuen | drama

LONDON • NEW YORK • OXFORD • NEW DELHI • SYDNEY

METHUEN DRAMA
Bloomsbury Publishing Plc
50 Bedford Square, London, WC1B 3DP, UK
1385 Broadway, New York, NY 10018, USA
29 Earlsfort Terrace, Dublin 2, Ireland

BLOOMSBURY, METHUEN DRAMA and the Methuen
Drama logo are trademarks of Bloomsbury Publishing Plc

First published in Great Britain 2024

Cover design: Jamie Jenkin/National Theatre

Photograph: Andrew AB Photography

A catalogue record for this book is available from the British Library.

A catalog record for this book is available from the Library of Congress.

ISBN: PB: 978-1-3505-0471-4
ePDF: 978-1-3505-0473-8
eBook: 978-1-3505-0472-1

Series: Modern Plays

Typeset by Mark Heslington Ltd, Scarborough, North Yorkshire

To find out more about our authors and books visit
www.bloomsbury.com and sign up for our newsletters.

George Caple	Snowy/Kevin/Scotty/Paper Boy
Dominic Carter	Malloy/Marley/Gas Man/Debt Collector/Shake-Hands/ Landlord/Catholic Priest/ Policeman/Groundskeeper
Helen Carter	Miss Sutcliffe/Freda/Margaret
Aron Julius	Loggo
Nathan McMullen	Chrissie
Lauren O'Neil	Angie/Jean/Lawton/Student/ Lollipop Lady
Jamie Peacock	Moss/Clerk/Redundant Worker/ Protestant Reverend/Milkman/ Understudy Snowy/Kevin/Scotty
Barry Sloane	Yosser
Philip Whitchurch	George
Mark Womack	Dixie
Understudies	Kieran Foster, Liam Powell-Berry, Hayley Sheen, Liam Tobin
Alan Bleasdale	Writer (Original)
James Graham	Writer (Adaptation)
Kate Wasserberg	Director
Amy Jane Cook	Set and Costume Designer
Ian Scott	Lighting Designer
Rachael Nanyonjo	Movement Director
Jocelyn Prah	Associate Movement Director
Dyfan Jones	Composer and Sound Designer
Kate Harvey	Associate Sound Designer
Jamie Jenkin	Video Designer
Sean Gannon	Head of Technical and Production
Rachel Bown-Williams of RC Annie Ltd	Fight Director
Carlotta De Gregori of RC Annie Ltd	Associate Fight Director
Lauren Dickson	Associate Director
Marie Jones	Wardrobe Supervisor
Andrew Lock	Technical Stage Manager

Helen Lainsbury	Company Stage Manager
Laura Thomas	Deputy Stage Manager
Alicia Southerton	Assistant Stage Manager

Boys from the Blackstuff was first performed at Liverpool's Royal Court 15 September 2023.

This version of the play was performed at Liverpool's Royal Court 19 April 2024, transferring to the National Theatre and then the Garrick Theatre in London's West End.

Boys from the Blackstuff

Characters

Chrissie, *thirties, Liverpudlian*
Yosser, *thirties, Liverpudlian*
Dixie, *forties, Liverpudlian*
Loggo, *twenties, Liverpudlian*
George, *seventies, Liverpudlian*

(The following roles can be taken on by the above or shared by the ensemble)

Angie, *thirties, Chrissie's wife*
Freda, *forties, Dixie's wife*
Snowy, *twenties, George's son*
Kevin, *nineteen, Dixie's son*
Margaret, *sixties, George's wife*

Miss Sutcliffe, *supervisor at the Department of Employment*
Moss, *'sniffer'*
Lawton, *'sniffer'*
Jean, *assistant*
Clerks

Malloy, *building contractor*
Scotty, *dock security*
Marley, *dock thief*
Paper Boy
Gas Man
Debt Collector
Shake-Hands
Landlord
Student
Catholic Priest
Protestant Reverend
Policeman
Groundskeeper
Milkman
Lollipop Lady
Neighbours
Customers
Redundant Workers

Prelude

A young man, **Snowy Malone**, *is falling slowly through the sky, against the sounds of violence, growing. A riot in the streets. Police sirens and angry crowds.*

He disappears into the darkness.

As the skies above Liverpool, 1982, emerge.

On the horizon is the River Mersey, and the sound of horns from the last remaining ships.

Act One

Scene One

The Department of Employment.

A line of men.

Chrissie   Christopher Todd.

Chrissie *in his own light, facing what we assume to be his* **Clerk** *at the counter.*

Voice of Clerk   *Full* name, Mr Todd.

Chrissie   Christopher *Robin*. Todd. (*Shrugs.*) It was me mam's idea.

We find **Loggo**.

Loggo   Loggo Logmond, and no offence like, but we've been through all this before.

We find **Dixie**.

Dixie   Dixie Dean.

Voice of Clerk   Any dependants, Mr Dean?

Dixie   Yeah, wife and four kids, two at school, two on the dole.

Voice of Clerk   Those on the dole don't count.

Dixie   Nobody on the dole counts, friend.

We find **George**, *who is wearing pyjama bottoms under his work jacket.*

George   George Malone.

Voice of Clerk   I'm not finding you, Mr Malone. Can I have your address?

George   228 Grafton Street, love.

All   Liverpool 8.

George   Come on, girl, I've been waiting half an hour. They'll be expecting me.

Voice of Clerk   Who'll be expecting you?

George   The *boys*. The boys will be expecting me. I mean there'll be ten ton of the blackstuff on the deck by now, and I don't like to let them down.

Voice of Clerk   Are you *working*, Mr Malone?

George   No. I just love watching people work. It's my fucking hobby.

And we find **Yosser**.

Yosser   Yosser Hughes. I'm Yosser Hughes!

Voice of Clerk   A test check is just a formality, Mr Hughes, but I'm afraid –

Yosser   Afraid? Y'll be terrified in a minute. Now sort me soddin' giro out before I knock you into the disability department.

Loggo   Yer wha'? Of course I want a job.

Loggo/Chrissie/Dixie/George/Yosser   Course I wanna job.

Loggo   I'm desperate, but you're not givin' me one, are yer.

Voice of Clerk   It seems, Mr Todd, that one of our inspectors has visited your house on two separate occasions during the past ten days without receiving any answer.

Chrissie   Ah what a shame.

Voice of Clerk   You were out?

Chrissie   Looks that way, doesn't it.

Yosser   My kids are here, my kids are right here, I've got my kids with me, do you understand that, pal?

Voice of Clerk   Mr Malone, have you been employed during this time? Look, have you got a job?

George   Me?

George/Chrissie/Dixie/Loggo/Yosser   No!

Chrissie   Oh yeah, I just come here for the company and the pleasant surroundings.

Voice of Clerk   When did you last work?

George/Chrissy/Dixie/Loggo/Yosser   A year ago.

Dixie   I remember the exact date, friend. The exact location.

George/Chrissy/Dixie/Loggo/Yosser (*ruefully*) Middlesbrough. Fucking Middlesbrough.

Voice of Clerk   You what?

Loggo   Forget it. Look –

Yosser   What's your name? You've got my name, I want your name. (*Leaning forward to look at a badge, presumably.*) 'Debbie'.

Loggo   'David'.

Chrissie (*leans forward to read his badge*)   'Ian'.

George/Chrissy/Dixie/Loggo/Yosser   I want a job.

Yosser   Gizza job. Go on, gizzit, go 'head, giz it if you've got it, giz it, I can do it. Giz it then. Go 'head, gizza job.

Chrissie   You know, you're meant to be the Department of Employment, so where's the employment? It's false advertising, that, you know.

Voice of Clerk   We'll be making a further visit to your house in due course, Mr Todd.

Chrissie   I'll bake a cake.

He goes. They all do, breaking off to reveal . . .

We follow **Chrissie** *into –*

The streets of Liverpool.

An Echo **Paper Boy** *arrives – or a man too old to be one – calling out the infamous phrase.*

Paper Boy   Echo, Exy Echo!

Exy Echoooo . . . Echo, Exy Echoooo.

Read all about it! Sky still blue, water still wet, Thatcher still a twat!

(*Gesturing* **Chrissie** *closer.*) Psst . . . I'm been sent by Frankie Malloy. He's got work at last, new contract, building site, cash in hand, nudge nudge wink wink.

He does the gestures, but the wrong way round, winking on 'nudge', and nudging on 'wink'.

Inside there. Details from Malloy.

Chrissie *reaches in and removes the envelope, slipping it into his jacket. At the paper –*

Chrissie   I'm not sure they fit anymore, those words. 'Liverpool' and 'Echo'.

Paper Boy   Why not?

Chrissie   An echo can bounce back.

He steps away.

To the streets and houses of Liverpool 8.

Loggo *exits his home holding a fishing rod and other gear, singing.*

Loggo
   Ol' man river
   That ol' man river
   He don't say nothing

But he must know something
'Cause he just keeps rolling!

Shouting over to what we assume to be **Neighbours** *watching, but could be directly at members of the audience . . .*

Alright there, neighbour? Me? Just off for a day by the water, that's all. Why else would I be lugging this lot about, ey. Only a mad man would do that if they weren't actually going fishing.

Chrissie *joins.*

Chrissie   Do you want to lay it on any thicker, Loggo. I bet you've never even used any of this gear.

Loggo   Yeah, when I was working up in the Shetlands. Nothing else to do.

Chrissie   Ever catch anything?

Loggo   Course.

Chrissie   What d'yer catch?

Loggo   Pneumonia.

They circle, passing **Dixie** *making his way home.*

Chrissie   Alright, Dixie? You coming or going?

Dixie   What are you, a sniffer now?

Chrissie   I'm just asking that's all, heard you got some nights somewhere.

(*As* **Dixie** *makes to continue.*) Come on, Dix, none of us have hardly seen yer since the – the thing, and –

Dixie (*turning on him*)   Wha', you mean when me and my boy got the sack because of you cowboys 'doing a foreigner'. Oh yeah, happy days they were, Chrissie, so glad to reminisce. Now frig off.

He goes.

Chrissie   Come on. Malone's house.

Loggo   Is George coming?

Chrissie   No, he's still in hospital. We're picking up one of his sons. Snowy.

Loggo   Ah not him! Not Karl Marx lives!

Snowy *joins, yelling at another* **Neighbour/Audience Member**.

Snowy   Yes, that's right, it's me again, love. Go ahead. Be a solid citizen. Do the decent thing and report me. Yeah, I'm going to work! For half my value. *That's* the disgrace right there, I'm telling ya.

Loggo   Christ, Snowy, why don't you just pay for an ad in the soddin' *Echo*!

Snowy (*pointing*)   It's her. Minge bag! The dole'll send flowers to her funeral, they will!

Chrissie   I'll grab me boots from mine and see you in the van.

He steps over, into . . .

The back yard of the Todd house. **Chrissie** *amongst his geese, pigeons and ferrets.*

Putting his work boots on, as **Angie** *comes out, a bustle of energy as ever.*

Angie   Right, I'm taking the kids to school, see how long either of them can stay out of bleeding trouble today, place your bets now.

(*Seeing his boots.*) Y'work boots? No-o, the dole had something for you, a job?

Chrissie   Not exactly.

Angie   . . . Oh don't bleedin' tell me.

Chrissie   Ang.

Angie   Suffering Christ; not that bleeding building site.
Taking cash in hand, when you've got the sniffers all over
yer? You're mad, you are, absolutely *mad*.

Chrissie   They're not all over me. They do it to everyone,
I'm not special.

Angie   I don't think you're special, Chrissie. Stupid maybe,
but –

Chrissie   It's only been a couple of visits to the door, it's
hardly the Spanish Inquisition.

Angie   Yeah and who has to answer the bleeding door
when you're not here? Lying through me teeth, and I hate
lying, I was never very good at it. So what do I say if they
come round for you today?

Chrissie   Tell 'em I've run off with a young model who fell
madly in love wi' me.

Angie   It's got to be plausible.

Who are you going with? Dixie?

Chrissie   No. I hear he's got something down on the docks,
and . . . he wouldn't work with us anyway. After
Middlesbrough.

Angie   He's stubborn. Like you. You were best friends.

Chrissie   'Best friends'; we're not children, Ang.

Angie   Oh, no. Children are full of life. Children – have
a *future*.

She heads off at pace.

Scene Two

Back at the Department of Employment.

Miss Sutcliffe, *the supervisor of the Fraud Section, in the offices
behind the counter.*

She arrives at a drinks station to top up a cup of tea, as **Moss** *passes.*

Moss   Ah, Miss Sutcliffe –

Miss Sutcliffe (*almost imperceptible sigh*)   Good morning, Mr Moss.

Moss   I'm glad I caught you –

Miss Sutcliffe   You haven't caught me, Mr Moss, I'm just acquiring some refreshment, very busy –

Moss   I'm good, me. Right? I just wanted to say that; I am, I'm good at me job. And I consider myself to be an asset, right, to this section, a resource that is not currently being exploited. I'm a natural at this, me, and –

Miss Sutcliffe   A 'natural resource'? Gosh, you sound like North Sea oil, Mr Moss.

Moss   I – I – yes, I am. I'm like North Sea oil. Only I'm not being tapped.

Just gimme something up my street. It's been weeks since my last assignment and –

Miss Sutcliffe   How long have you a fraud team investigator, Donald? Six months now? (*He nods.*)

It's a very delicate position we've been placed into. Isn't it? We are, after all, fellow citizens of this city. Our colleagues over in the Employment Section, their job – for the men and women queuing up to the counter – *their* job is to find *them* a job. But *our* job? Here in the *Un*-employment Section, our job is . . . well how would you define it, Donald?

Moss   Well. Our job is to –

Shifts in his seat.

Our job is to uphold the sanctity of the system. Uphold it by catching folk who are *cheating* that, erm, that system.

Miss Sutcliffe   To 'catch them'. Yes. Reluctantly, perhaps. Regrettably –

Moss   Yes, yes.

Miss Sutcliffe   And to do that, we rely on tip-offs. And tittle tattle. And tell-tales. People calling in with their suspicions. Neighbour turning on neighbour, families against friends. Perhaps one day turning on even your own family, your own friends, Donald. What might that do to a person's soul, I wonder.

Moss (*nods, getting it now*)   Right. Right, ok you don't reckon I'm capable –

Miss Sutcliffe   I didn't say that, I'm saying I don't know yet. What I'm saying, Donald, is that when it comes to you, I just don't know . . .

Don't look so worried, Mr Moss. Unemployment – is a growth industry. So much so that here, they're expanding. New premises, more staff. Which means as it happens . . . I think I *do* have just the job for you. There's a particular group we've been keeping tabs on. All in and around Liverpool 8.

Moss   Li– . . . Liverpool 8?

Miss Sutcliffe   Yes, Donald. Right – up – *your* – street.

She smiles, handing him the file, and leaves him to ponder it.

The building site. The **Boys** *are joined by the boss,* **Malloy***.*

Malloy   One short are we, then?

Loggo   Well, y'know what it's like. First sign of spring and all the boys pack off to their villas in sunny Spain.

Malloy   And who are you when you're out?

Loggo   I'm the brickie.

Snowy   Plasterer.

Chrissie   I'm anything you want me to be.

Malloy   Right, well there's that wall there, there's the blackstuff needs laying for a drive along here, the landscaping the garden there, plastering the walls in there –

Snowy   What's it going to be, this place? Ey it's not going to be a police station is it, because I'd have some objections to that –

Loggo   I'm happy not knowing, so's I don't get too emotionally attached, you know.

Malloy (*gesturing towards* **Snowy***'s ropes, slung over his shoulder*) I see you've brought your ropes.

Snowy   In case of a quick getaway is needed. Out the windows, and down.

Malloy   I shouldn't think the dole'll look for you here. You'll be alright.

As **Malloy** *is heading off,* **Chrissie** *hops after him.*

Chrissie   Mr Malloy? How, uh . . . how's it all going? Business?

Malloy   Oh. Fine thank you.

Chrissie   So you got a lot of work on, then?

Malloy   . . . (*Catching up.*) . . . Oh, well, not really. Not with this weather we've been having.

Chrissie   Yeah but weather can change I suppose, can't it, that's what the weather does. Even here –

Malloy   Look, I've really got to dash, y'know how it is.

He is about to exit, when –

Yosser   Oy!

Chrissie   Oh frig.

Yosser *arrives, walking with confidence and intensity.*

He will refer to his children often – but we never see them, often because he might appear like he's yelling at them at a distance.

Yosser   Gizza job, go on, gizzit, go 'head.

Malloy   A, a, a job?

Yosser   Yeah, gizzit, go on. I know you've got one, go on, gizzit.

(*Yelling to his children.*) Kids? You wait there! Maurice!

(*To* **Malloy**.) Alright to bring my children, innit, they're good kids.

Malloy (*looking to see them*)   Kids? On a building site? What kids?

Chrissie   Mr Malloy, I wouldn't –

Yosser (*at his children*)   Don't touch nothing, don't move nothing, don't *do* nothing – (*Back at* **Malloy**.) Yeah go on, gizza job.

Malloy   I'm only really looking for a brickie, today –

Yosser   Yes that's me, I'm a brickie. I can lay bricks.

Loggo   Yoss –

Yosser   Oh yeah. Oh aye, yeah. (*Back at the* **Boys**.) What?! (*Back at* **Malloy**.) Yeah, I can do that, oh too right yeah. I'm ready. (*Takes his coat off.*) I'm ready? Where is it, what?

Malloy   Well, I'll see how you . . . how you make out, then. Carry on that small wall, running parallel with his (**Loggo**'s).

Yosser   Right, right then, right you are, yeah right then.

He goes to the wall and begins slamming bricks down, getting his tools ready in a fashion.

Malloy (*to* **Chrissie**)   Do you know him?

Chrissie   . . . We used to.

Malloy *goes.*

The work begins.

The company roll their sleeves up/get changed and start, all the while singing along to their song.

Their first task is the laying of the tarmac for the path.

All (*singing*)
Oh, you can talk about the concrete,
And the boys who work the train
And the fellas in the hopper in the sun and wind and rain,
but the boys who work the blackstuff, sure they're really rough and tough
When they're working on the highway laying the old blackstuff.

Yosser *is slamming bricks down onto his wall in messy fashion, inelegantly scraping cement across them with a trowel and making a mess.*

Chrissie   Yosser.

Loggo   . . . Yosser? . . . YOSSER! You can't leave gaps like that.

Yosser   It's for ventilation.

They all place their rakes into a drum of flickering fire, spinning into –

The site hut for a tea break.

Chrissie   Brew? Fellas? Snowy? Tea? Loggo? You? Brew? Yosser? Tea?

All (*overlapping*)   Ay/yes ta/go on then.

Snowy   All I'm saying is, it was easy being a socialist when I was growin' up in the sixties. It was fashionable, and it was easy, cos times were good. But now it's gone sour and everyone's lockin the door, turnin' the other cheek, lookin' after number one. But this is the time we *should* be lookin' out for one another, innit. Now's the time to be together. Cos we're not winning anymore.

Loggo   Look I've paid me Labour membership, what more do you want?

Chrissie   Snowy pays for three, don't you? Workers Revolutionary Party *and* the Socialist Workers, too.

Loggo   No, but Snowy's different, aren't you, Snowy? Because you're the only one who is actually a worker in these so-called workers' parties. Amongst all those middle-class students and bleedin' Londoners.

Snowy   I can take it, y'know, Loggo. I can take it cos I know my beliefs are right. I've been bought up by me dad to support what's worth supportin'. I'm right. Aren't I, Yosser?

Yosser   Fuck off.

Snowy   Right.

Into –

All (*singing*)
    Oh we laid it in the harbour and we laid it on the flat
    And if it doesn't last for ever then I swear I'll eat my hat.
    I travelled up and down the world and over smooth and rough
    But there's not a surface equal to the old blackstuff!

Snowy *and* **Chrissie** *have started to plaster a wall.*

Snowy   I love doin' this, y'know. I'd plaster for nothing, if me principles'd let me. You know when you're doing something you're good at – there's nothing like it. Standing there in the morning facing four empty walls and then goin' home at night with the plaster all dry and smooth?

There, see? Ey, Chrissie, see that? I've even signed me name.

He's pointing in the corner. **Chrissie** *looks.*

Chrissie   Who do you think you are, Leonardo da Vinci.

Snowy   Why is my craft worth any less than his? 'Snowy Malone. 1982.'

(*Carrying on work.*) I can't stand those who take no pride. Like the sods who renovated this place the last time. You can see it. Shoddy. Rushed. Like them original tiles in the corridor out there, did you see the original tiles, Chrissie?

Chrissie   I've seen tiles, Snowy, lots of tiles.

Snowy   Beautifully made and precision laid, a hundred years ago. Until some bastard cracked them by putting up a tatty new banister.

I don't get jobs because I'm too good, and I do the job proper, and I'm slower than the bosses want me to be. So I'm not a profit margin, I'm now a liability.

Chrissie   Do you ever lose work because you talk too much?

Snowy   All right, but listen, Chrissie, I'm telling you, and I mean it; don't give in. Cos if you give in, you're dead. And I'm only tellin' yer cos I can see the signs.

Chrissie *considers this privately, before looking back at* **Yosser** *at his wall.*

Snowy   Still going bad, is it?

Chrissie   He's off his cake, Snowy. I don't know what to do. Ever since Middlesbrough.

Snowy   What happened in Middlesbrough? (*Waits, nothing, then.*) He went to see me dad, you know? Yosser.

Chrissie   Everyone goes to see your dad. You should be very proud of that. George Malone runs an unofficial surgery on Grafton Street for all the lost and frightened souls of this whole, cursed city.

Snowy   But Yosser turned up in the hospital, the other night.

Chrissie   The hospital? He can't even get a break there, your dad.

Snowy   And he sat with him for nearly an hour. Nurse had to ask him to leave.

Chrissie   'Kinnell. I don't know what to do with him. Honest to God. It's like talking to a brick wall.

A moment. They can't help share a slight smile.

Chrissie   Oh frig. Speak of the devil.

George *arrives onto the site.*

Snowy   Dad? Not again!

George   I'm fine, honest. I'm fitter than I've been for a long time, so they let me go, the doctors. Scout's honour. And I want to help. I want to work. I'm going out me mind, please, Chrissie, let me help you out, let me work.

Chrissie   . . . (*Sighs.*) Easy does it, then, right?

Into –

Laying the blackstuff again, moving the path further along.

All (*singing*)
　　We rolled it in the summer and we rolled it nice and hot.
　　But to roll it over all of this, we'd have to roll a lot.
　　I travelled up and down the world and over smooth and rough
　　But there's not a surface equal to the old blackstuff!

Into –

Another break. **Yosser** *is eating from a bag of chips, as* **George** *reminisces, as is his way, the others enjoying him, or at the very least listening out of respect.*

George   You know them down in London, in power and the press, they look at us up here, and they think that we're troublemakers. Right? That we're *difficult*. And they're not wrong. See my theory, and it's only a theory mind, but . . . the rest of our comrades in such and such towns, working in this and that, their lives are governed by the clock, see? But we're a *port city*. Our lives have always been governed by the *tide*.

Tides that ebb and flow, and have a life of their own. And that's it. That's the 'spirit' that's inside us.

Yosser   You sound like you've *had* a few spirits inside you. Haha.

George   I'm saying it's in all of us. (*Gestures to his heart.*) Young and old, it seeps through.

Snowy   I love that, Dad. The sea. Wild, and – honest.

George   Think of them. Those proud sea captains, who had their homes in Toxteth, in Victorian times. Men who travelled the world, bringing back all sorts great exotic things in their cargo holds. Because, you see, all the shipping lanes of the world led back here. Where we're standing, now. If you don't find that remarkable and then what do you?

Loggo   I don't know about Victorian times, George. I know that a year ago those same streets, where I live, where them sea captains once lived – they were on fire. In Toxteth. And I didn't see much proud then. I saw lots of bobbies, mind. Beating up my friends.

Chrissie   And that was bang out of order, Loggo; no one's saying it weren't.

Loggo   Fact one of the reasons I'm here in the first place . . . when you think about it . . . one of the reasons I'm here is because my ancestors would have been one of the 'exotic things', brought over, in the ship's hold. Me great-grandparents. Those shipping lane brought *me*.

George   Just stories, Loggo. What can I tell yer. Dockers are storytellers, always have been, always will be.

Loggo   Yeah shame they miss out some of the chapters in those stories though, isn't it?

George   Hey.

Loggo   And some characters too, good ones –

George   Heyyy, I was a *docker*, Loggo. Till the strike of '67, o'course . . .

Snowy   Yeah, the strike that *you* started. And led!

Chrissie   And got the sack for.

George   Oh yeah, well.

Loggo   I know that, George . . . I don't mean you.

(*Lightening the mood again.*) You got me my first real job, after all, in –

George   Oh yeahh! Ey but only cos y'bloody mother was stood there every night crying on me doorstep, begging me to try and get ya a job.

(*Mock-crying, back in his element.*) 'Just take him with ya!' That's what she said. 'Take him with you when you go away somewhere – far *far* away. The further the fucking better!'

Some laughter among the others now, even **Loggo**.

George   Ey and we went all over, kid, didn't we? All the great places. Ramsbottom.

Loggo   Hah. Spittal.

Chrissie   Urmston!

Yosser   Grimsby.

Snowy   Cockermouth!

George   Oy! Don't let your mother hear you talk like that!

He goes to collect mugs – touching **Loggo** *on his shoulder in passing . . .*

George   Right. I'll be the can-lady today.

Malloy *interrupts their break.*

Chrissie   Oh, Mr Malloy.

Malloy (*at* **Yosser**)   You do that wall?

Yosser (*chips in his mouth*)   What wall?

Malloy   The wall I asked you to do.

Yosser   Yeah, what about it?

Malloy   Come and take a look.

Yosser   I've seen it. Once you've seen one wall you've seen them all. (*Laughs.*)

Malloy   Hoh, not this one, this one's special.

Yosser   That good, ey?

Malloy   It's a disgrace.

Yosser   You leave my wall alone.

Malloy   Come with me –

Yosser (*snapping*)   Don't tell me what to do! No one tells me what to do!

A moment. The other men sense what's coming with dread.

Malloy   You're not a brickie, are you?

Yosser   I am. I've laid bricks before, anyone can lay bricks.

Malloy   Not since you had a Lego set! Go on – clear off. You're sacked.

Yosser   Sacked? Me – sacked? (*Laughs.*) How can you sack someone who's on the dole. (*Laughing harder.*) Sacking a man who doesn't even work for him! That's mad. That's a mad thing. That's mad, that, you're mad. Well give me my P45, then, if I'm sacked, go on giz it. Giz it.

Malloy   The only thing you'll be getting from me is –

Yosser *head-butts* **Malloy.** *He falls back.*

George   Yosser!

Malloy   Owh!

Loggo   What you doin', man?!

Yosser   My best. I was doin' my best.

Coat on, heading out.

It's a good wall, that. It's a good wall, last for ever that.

It's a good wall . . .

He goes.

Come on, kids! Maurice, get out of that cement mixer! Oy and put that hammer down, now! (*Exits.*)

Chrissie   I'm sorry, Mr Malloy –

Malloy (*standing, wiping his nose*)   He's not right.

Chrissie   Yeah, well, who is these days, you know?

(*As* **Malloy** *is going.*) Mr Malloy, I . . . I'm aware this isn't the best of timing, but –

Malloy   I'll talk to you tomorrow, Kenny.

Chrissie   Chrissie.

Malloy   Bright and early, all of you. (*Exits.*)

Snowy (*amused*)   Thought you were about to get down on your knees then, to your feudal lord, Chrissie. You'll be touchin' your forelock next.

Chrissie (*a moment, about to ignore it, but . . .*)   Do you know what, Snowy. I respect you. I respect your 'ideology'. But what you said earlier. People just lookin' after number one. You were right. People can't look far ahead these days, not when you're scared. Not when you're frightened. In the here and now. I can't feed my kids on principles and 'ideology'. I need money. That's it. I need money.

A moment. He starts to leave.

Loggo   See you tomorrow, Chris.

Chrissie   Yeah. 'Bright, and early'. For a job we haven't got.

(*Half-singing, bitterly, on his exit.*) 'But there's not a surface equal to the old blackstuff.'

Scene Three

The docks.

Dixie *wanders the docks with his torch. Horns sound.*

He checks his watch – bored, ashamed . . . and heads off after his shift.

Towards . . .

. . . the street.

Dixie *circles around, passing* **Chrissie** *and* **Loggo** *the other way brusquely, repeating their morning routine.*

Chrissie   Dixie.

Dixie   Christopher.

Chrissie *wavers briefly, wanting to say more to his old pal, but eventually carries on . . .*

Moss *and another 'sniffer'* **Lawton** *materialise, watching them all go.*

Moss (*into a handheld tape recorder*)   Suspects including Snowy Malone, son of George, and are heading in the direction of the site. I've followed him before. Little sod walked me all around town and then lost me in Mothercare.

He makes to go. **Lawton** *more relaxed, stretching, opening up a flask of tea.*

Moss   Hadn't we better get a move on, we'll lose 'em.

Lawton   Oh what's the use, we know they're going to Malloy's site, same as yesterday. I reckon that'll be enough to call in the back-up today.

Moss   Really? Right. (*Looking at where they went.*) So that'll be it for them, then?

Lawton (*rubbing*)   It's the knees, no one tells you about. All this hiding, crouching, kneeling.

Moss   It's the 'skulking' that gives me jip.

Lawton   Oh aye, the skulking's the worse. Still, it's a skill, to skulk well. It is.

Moss   This'll go down well for me, you know, back at the office.

Lawton   You think they care about *you*. We're anonymous footsoldiers, Donald. Doing the grunt work. Kept in the dark. Do you know I followed a bloke last month, followed him all day. Followed him, all the way to bloody court, and sat and watched him plead guilty to the offences I was bloody following him for! I'd been on sick leave when they pulled him in. Nobody thought to tell me when I got back.

We are not part of the bigger picture, Moss. Any more than they are.

Come on.

They head off to carry on their work. We stay on the street, and –

The Dean house.

Dixie *is calling up the stairs, as* **Freda** *sips her morning tea at the kitchen table.*

Dixie   Kevin? Kevin?! Get out that bed, you lazy git!

Freda   Oh what's he got to get up for?

Dixie   Because I told him to.

(*Opening letters in a huff.*) And I'm the only one allowed to go to bed in the day, because I'm the only one sodding workin', all night.

(*Slamming the letter down.*) Electricity.

Kevin *arrives, yawning.*

Kevin   What you yellin' at me for.

Dixie   Oh look, Sleeping Beauty's up. Well, don't expect a kiss, will yer?

Kevin   You what?

Freda   I'll kiss yer. 'Ere. (*Kiss him on the cheek.*)

Dixie   Look at the bleedin' time, it's a disgrace. You're not even trying anymore. Get out there and look for work. (*Slams another letter down.*) Gas.

Kevin   There is none.

Dixie   Gas?

Kevin   Work.

Dixie   There's none when you're lyin' in bed.

Kevin   And there's none when I'm walkin' up an down the industrial estate, neither! You know that, there's no point, so don't give me no crap about lyin' in bed.

Dixie (*reading the letter*)   Oh for God's sake. What are they *doin*'?!

Freda   Who? What's wrong now?

He hands the letter to **Freda**.

Freda (*reads*)   What do the dole want to see you for? You were there yesterday, what does it mean?

Dixie   Means I'm not going to bed, doesn't it! (*At* **Kevin**.) Go on, you have my sleep for me, why don't you!

He exits, into –

The street.

A moment alone, with **Dixie** *as he exits his home, hovering . . .*

Private grief, a temptation to go back inside with his family. Or knock on the door of an old friend.

Paralysed, lost, alone . . . he takes a breath and continues on his way, passing –

The door of the Hughes house. A **Gas Man** *is knocking.*

Gas Man (*at* **Dixie**)   'Scuse us, pal, you don't know if your neighbour's in at 13, do yer?

Dixie   What, see through doors now, can I?

Gas Man   Lights are on.

Dixie   Hah! Oh yeah. Yosser Hughes. Lights are on, yeah, but there's not been no one home for a while, friend, if you get my drift.

Yosser *answers.*

Yosser   Yeah what? What d'you want?

Sees **Dixie**. *Tries to get more a sense of himself, a breath . . .*

Yosser   A-alright, Dixie.

Dixie   . . . Yosser.

He goes, **Yosser** *watching him.*

Gas Man   Mr Hughes? . . . Mr Hughes?

Yosser   Yeah, who's asking?

Gas Man   The Gas Board.

Yosser   Oh yeah? Well, that's nice of 'em, to ask after me, dead nice, that is, do pass my thanks on from me, won't yer? Tell 'em ta very much for asking, very kind.

Gas Man   You're *late*.

Yosser (*checks his watch*)   Am I? What for? What have I got to be late for, is it a job? That'd be nice, that would, that'd be smashing, having something to be late for.

Gas Man   Is *Mrs* Hughes in?

Yosser   No. Mrs Hughes is not in. And the gas is in her name, so go and have it out with her. If you can find her.

Gas Man   I haven't got time for this.

Yosser   Why, are you late too? Ey, we're like that rabbit in that story, aren't we? What's that story? (*Shouting inside.*) Kids! What's that story with the rabbit?!

Gas Man   You're behind on your gas bill –

Yosser (*moving in on him*)   I know that. Course I know that, do you think I'm thick? Is that what you knocked on my door to tell me?

Gas Man   They'll cut you off, you know. Not my choice. I'm just the messenger!

He heads off at a pace.

Yosser *stands there seething, before stepping into –*

The Department of Employment.

The line facing out again.

Voice of Clerk   Name.

Yosser   I'm Yosser Hughes!

Chrissie   Christopher Todd.

George   George Malone.

Loggo   The Scarlet Pimpernel.

Voice of Clerk   *Name.*

Dixie   It's Dixie Dean, and I've been bloody summoned, right, so here I am; I'm here.

Voice of Clerk   Come through, Mr Dean.

The others watch him go. Into –

An interview room.

Miss Sutcliffe *and her assistant* (**Jean**).

Miss Sutcliffe   Thank you, Mr Dean. This is Jean. Jean, Mr Dean. She'll be –

Dixie   Alright, before we start, before we start, right, this is the second time running, the second time, right, that I've been called in, now what's the score?

Miss Sutcliffe   It's merely administrative routine.

Dixie   I can use big words too, you know. (*Thinks.*) Elastoplast.

Jean   Name?

Dixie   You already know it, you just used it yourself, so did he.

Jean   Name.

Dixie   Are you sure this isn't a trick question?

Jean   Name.

Dixie   Thomas Ralph Dean.

He starts pre-empting, overlapping her questions.

Jean/Dixie   Age.

Dixie   Forty-four.

Jean/Dixie   Date of birth,

Dixie   23rd of the third, 1938.

Jean/Dixie   Where do you reside

Dixie   47 Maryville Street.

Jean/Dixie   How long have you resided there?

Dixie   Fourteen years.

Jean   Are you/employed in any capacity?

Dixie   Are you resident at . . . (*Stops. Then.*) You've changed the order of the questions, that's not fair.

Miss Sutcliffe   Mr Dean –

Dixie   You're a cheat.

Miss Sutcliffe   Mr Dean, allow me to disabuse you of something. It has been some years now since I was presented with something even remotely original or found a glimmer of amusement in antics of this nature. Nothing can be gained from it. Please do realise that.

Jean   Are you employed in any capacity?

Dixie   Do you practise making speeches?

Jean   Are you employed in any capacity?

Dixie   Nah I never have the time, do I, I've always too busy comin' here!

Jean   Have you –

Jean/Dixie   – done any work since you last signed?

Dixie   No! Is your wife employed in any capacity, no! Are any other members of your family employed in any capacity, no! Do you keep budgerigars in the bathroom, no!

Miss Sutcliffe   Are you sure about that last question, Mr Dean?

Dixie   Yeah, they'd shit all over the place, wouldn't they.

Miss Sutcliffe   I meant about your wife.

Beat. **Dixie** *momentarily flummoxed.*

Dixie   My wife? What about her?

Miss Sutcliffe   Not being employed in any capacity.

Dixie   . . . Yes.

Miss Sutcliffe   Not even a bit of cleaning on the side, something like that.

Dixie   What did I say?

Miss Sutcliffe   Perhaps she wouldn't tell you. It can be very emasculating, when a husband isn't bringing home any money but the wife is.

A moment.

Miss Sutcliffe   Alright, thank you for your time, Mr Dean.

Another moment. **Dixie** *stands.*

Dixie   It's been a pleasure and an honour.

And goes.

Jean   There's nothing in the file about his wife, Miss Sutcliffe –

Miss Sutcliffe   I know. (*Standing.*) But there's no harm in putting the fear of God into some of them, is there? Keeps them on their toes. Follow up with a visit.

She leaves the interview room, bumping into **Moss** *and* **Lawton**.

Moss   Miss Sutcliffe.

Miss Sutcliffe   Donald.

Moss   We're ready to make a move. Malloy's site; Liverpool 8. (*Handing her a note.*) We'll need some back-up.

Miss Sutcliffe (*beat. She turns away, reading*)   So they really are?

Moss   I'm afraid so.

Miss Sutcliffe   And you've really got them.

So, that's really it, then . . .

A moment. The men not really sure what to make of her. She hands the letter back.

Miss Sutcliffe   Permission granted.

The docks.

Where **Dixie** *continues to moonlight as a security guard.* **Scotty** *arrives.*

Dixie   Alright, friend?

Scotty   I'm here now. You can go.

Dixie   . . . That's what I like about this job – the comradeship.

(*At his watch.*) Blimey, you're eager. Middle of the night, it's still my shift, isn't it?

Scotty *is looking around, being odd.*

Dixie   Do you even know what we're guarding in here, this boat?

Scotty (*shrugs*)   Some shipment to South Africa. Trainers, booze. What's it matter?

Dixie   . . . Doesn't matter, just . . .

Another bloke, **Marley**, *arrives.*

Dixie   Ey, what's all this then? Who's this when they're out?

Marley   No one, no one. Just a fellow traveller, you might say, a mutual admirer.

Dixie   Of what? Talk sense, I've been up all –

Marley   Of boats. Visiting boats, full of the world's wonders, but devoid of any real security.

Dixie   I'm the bleeding security, now hop it.

Scotty   He's just pulling your pisser, Dixie.

Dixie   You know each other?

Marley (*wandering*)   You know the best thing about boats that come into *this* dock? No containers. It's actually one of the things that did this city in of course, that's my economic theory anyway; want to hear it?

Dixie   No, I wanta finish me shift and go home, don't I, but –

Marley   See when shipping got containerised, after the war, them colourful loading bins you can lift from ship to ship, truck to truck? Our fate was sealed. The Mersey, you see, it's too shallow for them big boats, too thin. So up springs Dover and Southampton. And fucking Felixstowe. Huge docks, colourful containers for as far as the eye can see. Like rainbows. Well, here we don't get the rainbows, do we. Only the rain. (*Shrugs.*) That's it. That's my theory. Still, good for something, ey. Easy pickings.

(*Looking.*) What have we got?

Scotty   Cigarettes over there. Whisky, booze. Boots.

Marley   I'll get the van.

Dixie   You're out of your mind, they'll have you! They'll have me!

Marley   Have you not told him how this works?

Scotty   Look, Dixie, it's just how it is. All your predecessors, they got that into their head quite quickly. Otherwise it's their heads, unfortunately, that got done in.

Dixie   . . . Are you threatening me?

Scotty   Educating you. Helping you out.

Marley (*returns with some boots*)   Here. As a thank you.

Dixie   What are you doin'? I can't wear those, I'm the security guard!

Marley   It would make us feel happier, safer, if you did.

Dixie I won't be back tomorrow, if this is the deal yer know –

Marley Course you will. You're on the dole, aren't yer? That's why you can't run off and tell anyone, ey. They're on the make, employing you cash in hand. You're on the make too.

Dixie . . . I'm no thief. I just wanna keep me nose clean.

Marley Well, then, listen to me, Mr Clean, before y'think of looking down y'nose at us, let me tell you, the worst robbers on these docks are the so-called security guards. You're nothing. Yer the dregs, dragged here off the dole. So do what y'sposed to do. Stand there. And do – *nothing*.

A moment, as **Marley** *goes, him and* **Scotty** *beginning the theft.*

Dixie *left, holding the stolen boots. Doing nothing.*

The sun rises over the city . . .

Scene Four

The site, as the midday sun hits it.

Chrissie, **George**, **Loggo**, **Snowy**.

The blackstuff gets laid further and further along the path.

All (*singing*)
  Oh we laid it in the harbour and we laid on the flat
  And if it doesn't last for ever then I swear I'll eat my hat.
  I travelled up and down the world all over smooth and rough
  But there's not a surface equal to the old blackstuff!

Chrissie *interrupts* **Malloy** *as he passes through –*

Chrissie Mr Malloy? Quick word –

Malloy Very busy, Kenny, y'know.

Chrissie I'm not happy with the way things are. Fourteen pound a day –

Malloy   In your hand.

Chrissie   Yeah but it's not legal, is it, and things are bad for me down the dole, I've got sniffers callin' round me house and . . . what I'm saying is I want a job. A normal job. I know I'd be losing money, but I'd rather be legit and on less, than on more and . . . and not.

Malloy   Isn't this better than no job at all?

Chrissie (*beat. Nods*)   You don't want to take me on.

Malloy   If I took you on, what happens when there's no work. What, you want me to take you on and then lay you off, Kenny?

Chrissie   I wouldn't mind you using my real name.

Malloy (*remembering*)   Chrissie.

Chrissie   Yeah. Chrissie.

Malloy   I'm sorry –

Chrissie   Yeah yeah, so –

Malloy   Look, you're not listening. This is the building game, and this is Britain. In 1982. It's just . . . it's not worth it.

Chrissie   . . .

Malloy (*searching his pockets*)   Look. Here. Take a fiver –

Chrissie   I don't want your frigging charity, Malloy. I'm tired of being soft. I'm noted for it, you know. Why am I so – bloody – soft.

The sound of police/cars approaching at speed.

What the frig?

Loggo (*from elsewhere*)   Sniffers! Leg it!

(*As he runs.*) Snowy! SNOWY!

Everyone scarpers.

A chase as **Moss** *and* **Lawton** *arrive with 'help'.*

Snowy *finds himself against the edge of the ledge where he'd tied his ropes to the shoddy banister, as* **Moss** *arrives.*

Moss   Alright, don't be daft you, just give it up!

Snowy   I know you. I know you! You used to go out with me cousin! Y'live round here! Traitor! You're a traitor to your fucking class!

Moss   Come away from the ledge! Yer idiot! We've caught yer, right, just give it up!

Snowy   Adios, dickhead!

He tugs on the ropes as he lowers himself over the edge to escape.

. . . the rope snaps, giving way . . .

Chrissie   Snowy!

Snowy *'falls'.*

Silence.

His father **George** *watches . . . as though reliving it, in his mind . . .*

George (*singing*)
   . . . Get some sail upon her
   Haul away your halyards
   Haul away your halyards
   It's our sailing time . . .

We transition to –

The Green Man pub.

The men are putting on black jackets, for their wake. **George** *continues with his old sea shanty.*

George
   Get her on her course now
   Haul away your foresheets
   Haul away your foresheets
   It's our sailing time

Waves are surging under
Haul away down Channel
Haul away down Channel
On the evening tide . . .

Wife **Margaret** *joins* **George** . . . *handing him a walking stick. As he gradually ails further, being helped towards the pub.*

Margaret *is comforted by* **Angie**.

Chrissie *and* **Loggo** *sit, pints in hand.*

Dixie *enters. The other men look.*

He joins them, reluctantly.

Dixie   How's he doin? George?

Chrissie   Don't ask.

You're lucky, you could have been there, too. That was the job I asked if you wanted to come to, you said no. You'd have been caught by the dole too.

Dixie   Yeah, well, they're all over me anyway, so.

Is that it, for you lot then?

Chrissie   Being investigated. Decision pending.

Loggo   Head on the block, axe hovering.

Chrissie   Benefits stopped until they do.

Dixie   No benefits?

Sorry. That's rough, that is.

Chrissie   Yeah, well.

Dixie   No that's rotten.

'Investigation'. Who's investigating *them*, that's what I want to know. Who keeps *them* in check. Law unto themselves.

They drink.

Chrissie   'Shoddy renovation'. That's what he said. That's what did it for him: Snowy. His rope to climb out the window, he tied it to a cheap banister some cowboys had half-arsed to the Victorian tiles. He was right.

A couple of newly **Redundant Workers** *arrive, flashing some cash.*

Redundant Worker   Barman! Set 'em up will yer. We're toasting the end!

Margaret   I don't know those men, do I?

Angie   Oh Christ, sorry, Margaret. It's one of them redundancy parties. Ten a penny in the Green Man these days. Nothing else to do with the cash they've been given but piss it all away just to feel numb, briefly. I'll get 'em to quieten down.

Margaret   They're alright. Snowy would have wanted everyone to have a good time. He was a good boy.

I haven't been here since George became – . . . poorly.

It's changed. When did it become such a madhouse.

Angie   Good question. That fella there? That's Shake-Hands.

We find **Shake-Hands***, a bruiser who wanders the pub. He offers his hand to* **Loggo** *as he gets another round in.*

Shake-Hands   Shake hands.

Loggo   Please, not today –

Shake-Hands   Shake hands.

Takes **Loggo***'s hand. Beginning to squeeze . . .*

Margaret   He seems friendly.

Loggo   Argh!

Margaret   Oh dear.

Angie   Yeah not so much. And that's Joe, the landlord. He's aged twenty years in the past five, because he necks one drink for every two that he serves.

With the **Landlord***, serving* **Loggo***, having a whisky himself as he does.*

Landlord   The landlord over at the Rose and Crown, he keeps a shotgun under his counter. But I worry I'd use it on meself.

Tell y'. I'll be glad when I'm out of here. I've been due a move with the brewery for years, but they can't get anyone to come!

Redundant Worker   Cheers!

Landlord   There used to only be fights at the weekends and weddings. If they got legless before, they'd dance on the tables. Now they break them over each other's heads.

Back with the **Boys***.* **George** *sits at a table, next to* **Chrissie***,* **Loggo** *and* **Dixie***.*

Loggo   It was a nice service, George. We were just saying.

Chrissie   Yeah. We were.

George   Yeah.

Dixie   I'm sorry, George.

George   Ah.

Yosser *enters. A moment.*

Dixie   Yosser.

Yosser   Dixie.

Loggo   Alright, Yosser.

Yosser   Ay, Loggo, yeah.

Chrissie   . . . Dixie.

Yosser   Chrissie.

(*Then*.) Sorry, George.

George   Yosser.

Yosser   I'm sorry and that, you know.

George (*standing, looking at him hard . . .*)   Be warned. Yosser.
Behave.

Yosser *nods. They all sit.* **Angie** *clocks them all, by* **Margaret**.

Angie   Well, look at that. The Famous Five, back together.
Sometimes it takes a tragedy, doesn't it.

Margaret   Back together?

At the table . . .

George   Ey. When was the last time we were all . . .?

Chrissie   George?

George   You know.

Dixie   A year ago.

George   No. You sure.

Dixie   Oh yes. Very sure.

George   . . . Oh right.

Loggo   Yeah.

George   I remember now.

All (*dryly, at one another*)   . . . Middlesbrough.

*They stand – and begin, with the help of others – using the
paraphernalia of the pub, as though to tell a story. Which, after all,
is what pubs are for . . .*

Scene Five

. . . One year ago.

*A motorway service station café on the M62 – on the way to
Middlesbrough.*

Chrissie, **George**, **Loggo** and **Yosser** *with* **Dixie** *and his son* **Kevin** *on their journey east. A roadside full English. Buttering bread – smacking out tomato ketchup – slurping tea throughout.*

They are very much a friendship group here. **Dixie** *full of cheek.* **George** *is significantly healthier at this point.* **Yosser** *not yet the man he becomes.*

Dixie   Can't believe you brought your friggin' goose with you in the van, Chrissie, honest to God. Who brings a goose all the way to Middlesbrough. My happy-go-lucky nature has been seriously taken advantage of.

Chrissie   My Ang won't feed them when I'm not there; what am I meant to do, Dix?

Loggo   I thought you were on the sick, George?

George   No, just a little stomach bug, Loggo, I'm through it now.

Dixie   I mean it, if I find shit in the back of my van.

Chrissie   There won't be.

Dixie   Yeah, well. Before we set off again . . . I'll be having a gander.

(*Laughs.*) Ey? Awh come on, that was funny – awh you don't get it. The lot of you.

Loggo   We get it.

Yosser   So will his lord high and mighty be gracing us with a visit this time or what? Our great bossman?

Dixie   Wasted.

Yosser   Watching over us with a beady eye?

George   What's wasted?

Dixie   My comedy gold, that's what.

Yosser   I tell you what *is* wasted, our craft and hard work. The pittance we're getting paid for this. Wait till I phone the union.

Dixie   Ey, no, we don't want the union in our job, do we? You know the way we work – in, out, throw it down, get out. Union'd spoil that, wunnit.

Kevin   Where's Leeds?

Dixie   Y'what?

Kevin   Where's Leeds, Dad?

Dixie   What you goin' on about Leeds for?

Yosser   I'm only saying –

Chrissie   Dix, you gonna finish that sausage?

Dixie   What's it to you? What's everyone asking daft questions for this morning?

Yosser   I'm only saying, it's you and the boys, it's *you*, Dixie, who's made the bosses their dough, who makes them who they are, the Big I Ams. And what have you – what have any of us got out of laying the roads? Bugger all except passports and bad backs. Another fiver a day, that's what we want.

Chrissie   That sausage, Dix –?

Dixie   What about it?!

Chrissie   It's just I've got (*in his jacket pocket*), I've got my ferret in here, and –

Dixie   You're fer– . . .! He's brought his bleeding ferret in here.

Chrissie   Well, it's just I don't trust the geese, like. You know how it is.

Dixie   No, I don't know how it is!

Yosser   Because my missus and my two kids, they 'expect', you know. They have 'expectations'. And I don't mind that, because I have expectations.

George   Tell you what, Yosser, I'll give you another fiver a day if it'll give any of us some peace.

Yosser   And when they give us that fiver. That's when we ask for ten.

Dixie   You can't stop, you, can yer?

Chrissie   Dix –?

Dixie (*slamming his plate over*)   Here, have me sausage, here! Anything else I can do for you? Give it a massage?

Yosser   Ey, Kev, you heard about that? Massages.

Kevin   What about them?

Yosser   The types of hotels you stay in on jobs like this, when you're away. Somewhere to spend that extra fiver a day. A certain room, with a certain lady, relieving the stresses of the day for a certain price. (*Pretending to be massaged.*) Ooh, ohh that's it, love, that's it right there.

He laughs, as do **Loggo** *and* **George**.

Kevin   Is that true?

Dixie   Never you mind, son – Yosser, pack it in. Sometimes I think you want to cause trouble.

Yosser   Listen, dickhead. I've been around. I know the score. I've been down south, Saudi Arabia, Nigeria, the Shetlands.

Loggo   Ey, what's that like, the Shetlands?

Yosser   It's cold and full of ponies. Listen, Dixie, I've been around.

Dixie (*smiling, calm*)   Yeah, I know, Yosser. You've been everywhere and going nowhere.

Yosser   . . . Like hospital food, do yer, pal?

Chrissie   Look, Yosser, you're a good mate and all that, and I'm not being funny, but if the whole of Middlesbrough's going to be like this you might as well go home now. We don't like trouble in this gang.

Yosser   You know what your trouble is, Chrissie? You're too *nice*.

Chrissie *smiles, goes back to his tea/breakfast.*

Yosser   I'm not joking. It's almost enough to hate you for it.

Loggo/George   Alright, Yoss/Ey, calm down.

Yosser   I just want to make the job better that's all. For all of us.

A female **Student** *passes by, with a hitchhiking sign (turned away).*

Kevin (*bashfully*)   Alright?

Dixie   Leave her be, you.

Loggo   Alright, love, hitching a ride are we?

Dixie (*half at* **Kevin**)   Oh wait, let me guess, don't tell me. (*Hands to his forehead.*) Let me use me powers of deduction, and guess that you want to go to . . . *Leeds*!

She smiles, and turns the sign around. 'Leeds'.

Dixie (*arms out*)   Whey!

The others cheer and applaud his 'magic trip', teasing/ribbing **Kevin**.

Student   So are you going to give me a lift then, or not?

Kevin   Can we, Dad?

Dixie   I'll knock you to next Sunday in a minute, how's about that?

Yosser   Bloody students. Stop reading books, get a job, get some money and buy a rail ticket instead. Haha. Right, Loggo?

Dixie (*standing, getting ready to leave*)   Sorry, love. Van's full. (*To the* **Boys**.) Ey, and we've only got a 'poultry' amount of space as it is. Ey? (*Laughs.*) Ey?

George   That was worse than the fucking other one.

Chrissie   I'll just use the lav.

He leaves for the toilet.

George   And then we'd better crack on, hadn't we.

Dixie   Oy, I'm the foreman, George. I make the decisions here.

George   I am sorry, Dixie. Whatever you think.

Dixie   I think we'd better crack on. But that's me saying it, not you.

As they get ready to go. Jackets, etc. **Kevin** *edges over to the* **Student**.

Kevin   What are you studying?

Student   English literature.

Yosser   Pfffff.

Chrissie *is coming back, as* **Yosser** *leaps up to meet him, a private word.*

Yosser   Ey, Chrissie. Listen –

Chrissie   Oh, not this again, Yosser. I've told you, I'm not interested –

Yosser   No but listen, I've dug deeper on this, right. These other fellas in Middlesbrough, they're straight arrows. I have references. It's a proper job. They're paying cash.

Chrissie   . . . How much cash?

Yosser   1,700 square yards, right, at £1.60 charge per yard. They get a cut, 10 pence a yard. We're sound. Only . . .

Chrissie   Oh here we go, 'only' what?

Yosser   Well, they don't have the gear, so, like, we'd have to stump up ourselves to hire all that up front, like. But –

Chrissie   Oh yeah! Course we do. There's always a catch.

Yosser   No but listen, it's an *investment*, right? It's smart. What savings have you got?

Chrissie (*sighs*)   . . . I put a little aside, for a rainy day.

Yosser   See? Exactly, me too. This is the rainy day.

Chrissie   We'd have to sneak off the other site, it's doing a foreigner –

Yosser   For one day!

George   Leaving Dixie in the lurch; that's not on, that.

Yosser   We'd be *back*. And nearly two thousand pound richer. We're laughing then, aren't we?

Dixie   Oy, Tweedledum and Tweedledee, we're off.

Yosser   Alright, alright. (*Back to* **Chrissie**, *hushed*.) Only it's a four-man job, see, you'd have to twist Loggo and George's arm, too. Rope them in.

Chrissie   Why would I?

Yosser   They listen to you. Everyone likes you; likes Chrissie Todd. Don't leave me high and dry, don't leave me on my tod, Chrissie Todd, come on. This is it! This is our chance. Everyone's got to look after themselves in this world, this is what we'd be doing. I'm telling you, lah. It's *destiny*.

Chrissie   I'll think about it.

They head back to the table.

Student (*to* **Kevin**)   Do you study?

Kevin   Nah. Was gonna do music while on the dole. I play the guitar. But me dad got me into this, so.

Student   What is this?

Kevin   The blackstuff. Laying the roads.

Student   Is that what you want to do?

Kevin   It's not about wanting to or not wanting to, is it? It just is. You have to.

Student   You don't have to do anything.

Dixie   Alright, alright, listen University Challenge, you leave 'Universally Challenged' here alone, pumping his head full of crap. (*His watch*.) Come on.

Yosser   You know your trouble? Girls like you?

Student   No, go on, what, I can't wait.

Yosser   You'll never be happy. You don't know what position you want in life, you think you're too good to change nappies and cook chips, so you'll always be off, searching for something else, something 'better' and never be happy.

Student (*smiles*)   I've got a brother like you at home.

Yosser   Oh aye. Good looking, is he?

Student   No, he suffers from the same thing though.

Yosser   What thing?

Student   What you are.

Yosser   What am I? 'Ere hold up everyone, wait for this, I'm about to be diagnosed! By a student! I'm about to be cured. Go on then, lah, what am I?

Student   Scared.

A moment. No one knows quite what to say as **Yosser** *seems to forget to smirk this off, shifting a bit on his feet, before coming back to his usual self, sneering*

Yosser   'Scared'. Hah.

Student   Yeah.

She goes. **Yosser** *laughs.*

Yosser   Scared! (*Imitates being scared.*) Oh no, eek, ahh. Tart.

Dixie   Come on.

They go. **Yosser** *looking back briefly at the* **Student**, *who disappears the other way.*

As the world of the pub returns.

Yosser *getting his surroundings back, in his mid-, dream-like state.*

Shake-Hands   Shake hands.

Yosser   . . .

Shake-Hands   Shake. Hands.

Yosser *offers his hand. They shake.* **Shake-Hands** *squeezing. Struggling.*

Until **Yosser** *head-butts him, and* **Shake-Hands** *falls back onto the floor.*

Shake-Hands   Pint of bitter for the boy.

Angie *and* **Margaret** *return from the bar.*

Margaret   George won't even talk about it, you know. And I've learnt not to ask what happened.

Angie *seems to move through all the different* **Boys**, *as she finishes the story herself . . .*

Angie   They lost their bleeding minds, that's what happened.

She faces and or wanders near to the **Boys**, *one by one, as she references them. They're in their own world almost, staring out . . .*

To **Yosser** *first.*

Angie   When they were up there, tarmacking this new estate, they got tempted into this moonlighting on the side by some shady fellas. Behind Dixie's back. They knew he'd say 'no'. So the world's greatest minds, here, withdraw all their savings to buy their own gear.

Yosser *turns away.*

Angie   Even George, can you believe. Wanting to believe the best in people, as always . . .

George *turns away.*

Angie   Only the shady fellas do a runner with the money, of course, leaving them high and dry. Screwed over on that fake job, fired from their real one.

Including – Dixie, as the foreman. Always responsible for everybody else.

Dixie *turns away.*

Angie   And me and Chrisse, we lost everything, didn't we. Everything we'd worked hard for and saved . . . Living hand to bleeding mouth ever since.

Chrissie *turns away.*

Margaret   Such bad luck.

Angie   Bad luck. Yeah. Maybe. Some people make their own bad luck.

She turns away too as . . .

. . . day turns into night, and the pub is alive again.

Everyone *several drinks down as, in one corner, the redundancy party is having a sing.*

Redundant Worker
  We're on the one road,
  Sharing the one load
  We're on the road to God knows where . . .

  We're on the one road,
  It may be the wrong road,
  But we're together now, who cares!

Malloy *enters.* **Angie** *clocks this first.*

Angie   Now this visitor, he *is* unwelcome. I'll see to this, Mrs Malone.

She faces up to him.

Angie   It's Mr Malloy, isn't it? Can I help you?

Malloy   I just wanted to pay my respects.

Angie   You should have just paid them a legal wage, then we wouldn't be here, would we?

Chrissie (*intervening*)   I've got this, Angie.

Angie (*shakes her head at him*)   Oh yeah, I bet you have. I bet.

She leaves them to it, watching from afar.

Malloy   I'm sorry, Chrissie. He was a good lad. Good worker.

Chrissie   He was. And he was proud of it, too. Is that all you came to say?

Malloy   Well. Only that, I uh . . . look, I'm also getting my wrists – you know . . . being charged, by the – for all the trouble and that.

Chrissie   We're all gonna be charged, Malloy. We don't get let off just cos our friend died. And you don't get let off just cos you're the boss –

Malloy   It's just, one of the things I told them was that I'd just started you all on, that week, and I was in the process of getting your P45s sorted. So . . . so if you backed me up –

Chrissie   Come on, not here, right?

Malloy   Please, Chrissie, Christopher –

Chrissie (*tragic laugh*)   Oh you know my name now, alright, well –

Malloy   This could ruin me –

Chrissie (*nearly snapping*)   Well! . . . (*Aware that others are looking. He calms.*) That's all that's left here, anyway, isn't there. Ruins. Join the club . . .

He sits at **George**'s *table.*

Malloy *– uncertain – goes to the bar, hovering.*

Moss *sees him, and turns away, avoiding his eye.*

Malloy   Evening.

Moss   Hello.

(*Going over to* **George**.) Look I just wanted to say . . .

George *glares at him, standing, and* **Moss** *moves away.*

Chrissie   Pay no attention, George.

George   . . . My boy, Chrissie.

Chrissie   Yeah. I know.

George   The things you . . . you plan to pass on. Leave behind. Where does that go, now?

Chrissie   Where does that go?

George (*looking around the pub*)   I don't know, Chrissie. I do wonder . . . That 'spirit', that seeps through. Generation, to generation. I look around . . .

Chrissie   George.

George   Snowy had it. He would've . . . after me. For the people, round here. He . . . But now. Who's going to?

Chrissie   Who's going to what?

George *looks at* **Chrissie** *now.*

George   Where is everyone? Where are *you*, Chrissie Todd?

Chrissie   . . . Me? I – . . . (*Looking down.*) I'm just passing through, George. Like everyone, not here to change the world, fly any flags, I'm just getting through.

George   Where *are* you . . .?

A moment. Then . . .

I could do more. I will do more.

Chrissie   George, no, not you, you're –

Malloy (*coming over, awkwardly*)   Chrissie.

Chrissie (*standing, approaching*)   Not now, I said not now.

Malloy   I'll give you a job.

Chrissie   You what?

Malloy   A *real* job. That's what you wanted, isn't it? If you have that word, with the dole. Like we said.

Chrissie   Not like this.

Malloy   All legit, starting now.

Chrissie   You can't just . . . here, like this.

Malloy (*offering his hand*)   We can shake on it, go on.

Chrissie   I . . . I don't . . . I . . .

Chrissie *looks at the hand extended out to him. Feels* **George** *watching.*

Chrissie   Not here, right. Just not here.

He goes back to the table.

Malloy   Right, so you'll think about it.

Chrissie   I didn't say that. I . . .

Malloy   Job's yours if you want it.

Yosser   A job?

Chrissie   It's nothing.

Yosser   I'll have it. Giz that job, giz it.

Malloy   It's up to Chrissie.

He exits the pub.

Yosser   What's up, Chrissie? What's up, Chrissie? That job? I'll have a job.

Chrissie   I don't want it. I can't.

Yosser   Don't want it? Take it. Take that job.

Chrissie   George, what you were saying . . .

Yosser   Giz that job, take that job. Chrissie, giz it! Take it! That's a job, that! That's a job!

Chrissie   I know, Yosser. Just . . .

George   What's this?

Chrissie   It's nothing, George.

Yosser   Take it!

Chrissie   I . . .

George   Chrissie?

Chrissie   I can't.

Yosser   Can't?!

He punches **Chrissie**.

Dixie   Ey!

The pub erupts – **Dixie** *and* **Loggo** *trying to hold* **Yosser** *back.*
Angie *coming over to* **Chrissie** *on the floor.*

Angie   What are you playing at?! Not here!

Yosser   I told you, Chrissie! I've always told you.

You're too *good*. You're too soft to survive.

And you're always going to be frigging happy, aren't yer
. . . ? AREN'T YER?!

You gonna go through life content. And easy going. And
above all *happy*.

Yeah you don't want nothing, do yer.

Any of yer!

You don't want to be rich. You don't want to be somebody.

All my life I wanted to be somebody.

I want to be noticed, Chrissie, I want to be someone, I want
to be seen. I AM A HUMAN BEING! I'm alive, I'm here
now, LOOK AT ME!

Chrissie   . . . I don't want to be somebody, Yosser. I'm
already me.

*A moment between them. As the world of the pub begins to fade,
leaving only –*

Chrissie. *Alone in the darkness.*

As, like **Snowy** *at the top, he begins to fall gently, through space . . .*

Interval.

Act Two

Scene One

Yosser *is falling through space . . .*

He wakes up, screaming in his bed.

Yosser Aaagghhhh!

Maureen? Maure – . . . (*He remembers. Then.*)

Kids? KIDS?!

Where are you? Get in here.

That's right. Climb in, that's it. All in, together.

I'm ok.

Are you ok? Hands in the air everyone in this bed who is ok?

Good. That's good. We're having a good time, aren't we?

A moment. Calmer, now . . .

I love you. Yeah . . .

I was in love with meself for a long time. Years and years . . . but I always knew it was a love that would not last.

Tries to laugh. Then . . .

When you were born, you know.

When you were born. I mean when you were born. Then it was . . . hah, it was uh . . .

I was alright, then.

Wait? Wait, what time *is* it?

(*Looks at his watch.*) I'm late. I'm late!

He leaps out of bed, to leave . . .

We find – the doors or entrances to three homes: the Hughes house on our left, the Dean house in the middle and the Todd house on the right.

The central Dean house has a front door to the left, back door to the right and a telephone in the middle.

Dixie *is getting ready to leave.* **Freda** *here.*

Dixie   You're not going out leafleting today, Freda; they knew. I'm telling yer. Someone's blown you up.

Freda   But who'd do a thing like that, round here?

Dixie   More people than you realise. The world is not what you think no more, girl.

Freda   It's only a pound an hour, three afternoons a week.

Dixie *(upwards)*   Well get *him* out of bed, looking, then! He has no respect. Never has.

Freda   You really are friggin' clueless you, aren't yer?

Dixie   Ey?

Freda   'Respect'? He used to sodding worship you.

Dixie   . . . Oh. Givin' me that, sod off.

A brief moment here, though, for **Dixie** *. . .*

Freda   Oy, where'd you get them boots?

Dixie   They fell off the back of a boat.

Freda   I'll have to go tell the girls I'm not coming then, I can't just leave them.

Dixie   You don't get it, do you! That's just what they want! Bad man with binoculars sees you meet other girls. Bad man follows nice girls, sees nice girls putting leaflets through letterboxes for a pound. Makes bad man happy!

He's lost his temper more than he meant to. A breath.

Freda   I'm not completely soft, you know. Before you went on the docks, we needed the money I got with the girls, it was the only money we had.

Dixie   . . . Listen. If anybody comes sniffing round, you don't let 'em in y'hear? You don't open that front door! You don't open that *back* one! They're watching.

He leaves.

At the Todd door.

Chrissie *about to leave,* **Angie** *berating him.*

Chrissie   Oh, we talked about this!

Angie   No. No, we didn't talk about it. You threw a moody and went out there to talk to the animals. I married Doctor friggin' Dolittle.

Chrissie   Three slices, three stale slices.

Angie   Yes and gave them to your bloody geese, and it was the kids' breakfast!

Chrissie   They were stale!

Angie   Everything in this house is!

Chrissie   Oh beautiful, that's just *beautiful*, that.

He exits, leaving **Angie** *pacing around, angry.*

On the doorstep of the Hughes house.

Yosser *exits at speed, only to find –*

Gas Man   Gas man.

Yosser   Not now!

Gas Man   You're behind, Mr Hughes –

Yosser   I KNOW! I know I am, why are people always tellin' me things I already know!

Gas Man   They'll be coming here, Mr Hughes. They'll be coming to take things.

Yosser   Take what? There's nothing to take. Only thing they could take is the piss. That's all. That's all that's left. Are you taking the piss?

Gas Man   Look, I am human. I do get it. You don't have a job.

Yosser   I did have a job. I *could* have a job.

(*Realising*.) You have a job. Giz it. I could do that. I could be a gas man. I could knock on doors and show my badge and ask for money from folk who don't have any, I could do that. Giz it. Go on, oh go on, giz it.

Gas Man (*retreating now, slightly*)   Mr Hughes.

Yosser   Go on, gizza job, giz it!

At the Dean house.

Angie *arrives at the front door, knocking, looking around carefully.*

Angie   Freda? It's Ang. I was wondering if I could tag along, leafleting with you and the girls today. I need anything I can get.

Freda *gets on her hands and knees and crawls to the door.*

Freda   Angie, stop knocking, will you, we think they're watching.

Angie (*through the letterbox*)   What are you doing? Who's watching? The dole?

Freda   They had Dixie in again, they were asking after me, it's not safe. And isn't your Chrissie under investigation anyway? They could be watching him!

Angie   Oh don't worry about him, he doesn't leave the house for nothin', now.

Chrissie *arrives at* **Freda**'s *back door, knocking quietly.*

Chrissie   Psst! Dixie?

Angie (*not hearing this*)   And if he ever asks, don't tell Chrissie I was here.

Freda *is crawling on her hands and knees to the back door now.*

Freda   Who's that?

Chrissie   It's Chrissie. I just . . . I want to speak to Dix, Freda; it's daft us going on like this.

Freda   He isn't here, go away.

Chrissie (*sighs*)   Alright.

Through the front-door letterbox –

Angie   Freda?

Freda *starts crawling back to the front.*

Freda   What?

Through the back door –

Chrissie   Freda?

Freda (*turning*)   What?!

Chrissie   Don't tell Ang I was 'ere.

He leaves.

The phone rings.

Freda *crawls to that.*

Freda   2033?

Voice   Is that *Mrs* Dean?

Freda   No, it's the Queen of friggin' Sheba; what?!

Angie (*through the letterbox*)   I'll leave you to it then, Freda.

Voice   Tell your husband, his pals rang. From the docks.

Freda   Tell him what?

Angie   Tell Dixie to swallow his pride and come round, for Chrissie, will yer?

Freda (*at* **Angie**)   Tell him what?

Angie *leaves.*

Voice   If he doesn't play ball tonight, I might be paying *you* a visit instead.

Freda   . . . I beg your pardon?!

The line goes dead.

Malloy *has turned up at the back door, knocking.*

Malloy   Hello?

Freda *crawls to the back door.*

Freda   Who is it, now?!

Malloy   It's Frankie Malloy. I need Dixie. I'm in a bit of a pickle with Chrissie. I wondered if Dix might pop round and have a word.

Moss *arrives at the front door, knocking.*

Moss   Mr Dean? Mrs Dean?

Freda *is crawling towards the front door.*

Moss   I'm from the Department of Employment?

Freda *stops, panicking.*

Freda   Oh frig,

Malloy *loudly, through the back door –*

Malloy   There's some work in it, for Dixie. Cash in hand!

Freda (*spinning back*)   Ssh! The dole!

Malloy   No I swear, the dole wouldn't have to know anything about it!

Freda   Shut the frig up!

The phone rings She answers.

Freda   What, *what*?

Jean (*hissing on the phone*)   Mrs Dean? It's Jean. From the office of employment?

Freda   Who is it?!

Moss/Malloy   Donald Moss!/Frankie Malloy!

Jean (*on the phone*)   Jean. I'm ringing to inform you that . . .

Moss (*overlapping*)   Mrs Dean?

Malloy   Freda? Freda?

*As **Freda** is spinning around on her hands and knees, getting caught up in the phone wire.*

Freda   What the bloody hell am I doing? Look at me. This is what they do to yer, isn't it?

Moss/Malloy   Mrs Dean?!

Freda   FUCK OFF!

Moss *slinks away.* **Malloy** *slinks away.*

*A silence, as **Freda** catches her breath. Broken by . . .*

Jean (*on the phone*)   Mrs Dean? –

Freda   And you can sod off too! And take your stupid soddin' voice with yer!

Jean (*on the phone*)   I'll have you know I'm taking elocution lessons –

Freda *slams the phone down.*

*Just as . . . **George** arrives, increasingly weak, at the back door.*

George   Psst.

Freda   Oh fuck me sideways, who's this now?!

George   Dixie . . .? Freda . . .? I just wanted to warn you. The sniffers are snooping around.

Freda   I know that! I . . . (*Realising*.) George?

She stands and opens the door, helping him in.

George, come in. Hell's teeth, how are you?

George   I . . .

Suddenly, he vomits up blood. Struggling to his knees.

Freda   George?!

She runs to the phone and dials.

George   I've made a right mess of your kitchen carpet, Freda . . .

Freda   Ambulance!

We fade to the sound of an ambulance approaching . . .

The Department of Employment.

The **Boys** *in their queues.*

Chrissie   Chrissie Todd.

Voice of Clerk   Your *full* –

Chrissie   Christopher Robin Todd.

Loggo   Loggo Logmond.

Dixie   Dixie Dean.

Yosser (*rushing up*)   I'm here! I'm here now, I'm here, aren't I. Yosser Hughes.

Chrissie   I'm being investigated.

Voice of Clerk   Say again.

Loggo   I'm under investigation.

Chrissie And I wondered if any decision had been made, you know. I'm kind of in limbo, here.

Voice of Clerk You'll be informed of the outcome in time, Mr Todd.

Chrissie 'In time'. 'In time' for what?

Yosser Oy! Chrissie!

Chrissie Oh frig . . .

Yosser Take that job!

Chrissie Not now, Yosser. (*Leaving*.)

Yosser Ey! He shouldn't be here! He's been offered a job! Oy, you. Take that job, or giz that job. Take it. Giz it. Are you going to take it?

Chrissie It's – guilt money. A guilt job.

Yosser Well, then, giz it. Giz that job.

Voice of Clerk Excuse me, sir?

Yosser Oy. They're expecting me. I am expected! I'm Yosser Hughes.

Voice of Clerk One moment, Mr Hughes.

The Fraud Section.

Miss Sutcliffe *in her office.* **Yosser** *sitting down.*

Yosser Yeah, what then, what's all this about then, what? I've got my kids here, can't you see I've got kids.

Miss Sutcliffe Mr Hughes, we *have* talked about your – 'children', before –

Yosser What about them, they're my kids, mine, you leave them, right. They're not going anywhere. They can stand outside, but with the door open, right?

Kids, come here!

He leads them to outside the door and arranges them so that they are in a line and facing into the office. He re-enters, and **Miss Sutcliffe** *is about to close the door.*

Yosser   You leave that door open! I want my eyes on them at all times – kids?! Eyes on me at all times, eyes forward, face forward, face me.

Miss Sutcliffe *sighs and goes to her desk.* **Yosser** *faces outside the room for the entirety of this exchange, back to her and* **Moss.**

Miss Sutcliffe   It's regarding the incident on Mr Malloy's building site. Were you employed by Mr Malloy around the time of the incident?

Yosser   Right, well, right, so, on Malloy's site on that particular day, the day in question, no money parted company with anyone, to or from anyone, who was there, while I was there, no money came my way, not that I was there. And I should know. Because I was there. Being me. Malloy on no occasion never said to me, here ya', touch for that.

And, as a matter of fact, I was there on a trial basis only, but left after, after a wobbly wall, and short exchange of words.

He pulls a few silly faces for his kids.

Miss Sutcliffe   Look, Mr Hughes, if you could –

Yosser   Look, here I am! A man!

Haha . . . 'a man'. A man with no job. Looking for one.

Have you got a job, giz a job, ey. Ey. I'd be alright if I got a job. I'd be alright. Oh yesssssssssssss. Oh yes.

The intercom buzzer sounds.

Miss Sutcliffe   Cue the inevitable heavy breathing.

She presses the button.

Yes, Jean?

Heavy breathing before she speaks. **Miss Sutcliffe** *indicates 'what did I tell you?' to* **Moss.**

Jean (*off*)   Miss Sutcliffe? Mr Logmond to see you.

Miss Sutcliffe   That'll be all, Mr Hughes.

Yosser *disappears from the office.*

And **Loggo** *appears in his place.*

Loggo (*at* **Moss**)   He shouldn't be here.

Miss Sutcliffe   Mr Logmond –

Loggo   It was him.

Moss   Careful you, careful.

Miss Sutcliffe   Our *intention* currently is to forward your papers for prosecution.

Loggo   So you are gonna do us then?

Miss Sutcliffe   It means I am trying, desperately trying, to find a satisfactory explanation. So that lessons can be learned.

Loggo   Well, while you're learning, I'm not earning. You've got me benefits on stop. But by all means, do take your merry time.

Moss   Now listen.

Loggo   What lesson is there? There's no lesson. It doesn't make sense, and it isn't meant to. We go round and round, chasing each other, and getting nowhere. Like gerbils on a wheel in a cage.

You're in it, too. That's the funny thing. You think because they give you a badge, that you're above it all but you're not. You're in here with us. Going round and round and round.

Moss   None of this is helping, you know. Why don't you *help* yourself?

Loggo?   Why?!

The state of it . . . the *state* of it . . . Screw you. Alright. Go on. Go 'head. Do what you please. See if I care.

Stands, goes to leave and stops.

I wouldn't be you. I wouldn't *be* you . . . Not for anything.

He goes.

Scene Two

The Malone house.

George *in his armchair, conducting one of his informal 'surgeries'. His visitor today?*

Yosser, *sat opposite.*

Yosser   They're gonna take 'em from me. But they're all I've got.

Might as well, they've taken everything else. *She* took everything. She did. Oh yes.

(*Then.*) Say something, George, go on, please.

George   . . . You fucked up my son's funeral. Yosser. I would *never* – . . .

Yosser   Yeah, sorry. I'm sorry about that. I am.

George   Yosser, you're not well. (*Shifting in his chair, in pain.*)

Yosser   *You're* not well.

George   No. My stomach. It's all gone.

Yosser   Haven't got the stomach for it, ey? Can't stomach all this anymore.

George   You might be right there.

(*Then.*) You seen Chrissie on your travels?

Yosser   Chrissie? Yeah I see him. Doesn't wanta see me, though . . .

I want my children.

That's what I want. I want my kids, but . . .

George   Go to the social services, and talk quietly, behave properly, explain your position. Show them where you live and how you're living.

Yosser   I haven't got a chance, then, where I live, how I live, have I?

George   . . . Ok. Yosser. Ok. Let me tell you, this. You know Hope Street?

Yosser   Hope Street? Yeah.

George   I've always liked that road. That road that cuts right through the middle of this city. And not just because it's called Hope, though that too. But because of what it represents. At one end, you've got the Catholic church. Paddy's Wigwam.

Yosser   Paddy's Wigwam, yeah.

George   And down the other end, is the Protestant cathedral. Right.

Yosser   Right, yeah. Yeah. What's your point?

George   I'm saying . . . that's what makes it Hope Street. That there are different ways to be saved. No matter who y'are.

Yosser   Why do you know everything?

George   Why do I –?

Yosser   Why do people come to you? I couldn't do that. What you do. I couldn't do that job, me. Don't give me that job, I couldn't do it.

George   I know hardly anything. I just try and apply the little bit I know, and what I learn, to some useful purpose. That's all.

Yosser   I want to be like that. I want to be someone . . . just that.

George   Be yourself, Yosser. That's all. Just be yourself.

Yosser *gets up to go, stopping briefly.*

Yosser   But what happens if you don't like yourself.

A moment.

Ok, see ya, George.

He heads off fast.

George   See you, Yosser. (*Once he's gone.*) Wouldn't wanta be you.

The next 'visitor' arrives –

Dixie *sat here sullenly. Reluctantly.*

Dixie   I don't know what to do. And I've always known what to do.

I resent it, George. I resent having to sneak about in the dark. Like some . . .

I want to be clean. I want to be *good*. But it's like – they won't – let me.

My dad brought me up to be proud, proud of hard work. Proud to put your overalls on, on a Monday. Proud to put a suit on, Friday. Go out. Behave proper. Have respect. That's what it is, that's what they *take*, it's the *respect*, it's . . .

What respect am I teaching *my* boy, ey? He's not gonna be sat talkin' in ten years' time about what *his* old man taught *him*, is he? What have I bleedin' . . .

George   Look. What is it really? Dixie?

Dixie   . . . Ahh, I shouldn't even be here, I'm sorry –

George   You're alright, Dix. Y'can always come and see me.

You don't ever see Chrissie, do yer?

Dixie   No. And the feeling's mutual.

. . . But I – I miss him.

Pause.

There. Right?

I miss my pals. I miss havin' my friends around. Working together, being togeth – . . .

But I have so – much – *anger*. And what they did, to me. I'm not blamin' you.

George   You can blame all you like, Dixie.

Dixie   I just still feel *so* . . .

(*Calms. Quieter now.*) I still feel so betrayed.

George   . . . I'm sorry, Dixie. I truly am. But. It sounds like you're doing the best you can. Yes, you're making 'compromises'. We all are. But you can still walk with your head held high –

Dixie   High?! Hah. I've never looked at my feet so much.

Are you sleeping? I can't sleep. I feel like I'm in a constant state of not being awake or asleep, like nothing feels real.

George (*nods. Then*)   Have I told you my theory? About why it's us. This city, they're trying this out on. It's the tides. We don't operate on clocks. And so they think we're troublemakers –

Dixie (*stands, now*)   Yeah, yeah, yeah, I've heard 'em all, George, no disrespect, every bugger out there wants to tell me why it's 'us'; why it couldn't be helped, why it's all inevitable. The bleedin' tides, friggin' containers, the Mersey's too deep, we're too far north, not far enough; history, politics, economics. Do you wanna know what it is? What it really is?

We're facing the wrong bleedin' way! That's all. Nothing more, nothing less, no meaning to it. We're on the wrong side of the bloody country. When it was America doin' all the trades, we were made. Now it's all gone to Europe. Trade. And we've been caught facing in the wrong bloody direction, looking the wrong way.

And don't I know how *that* feels!

He exits. We follow him . . .

Into –

The street.

Dixie *passes* **Yosser**.

Yosser   Come on, kids! We're going sightseeing! Going into town.

He starts marching, playfully/intensely, singing along to an old children's song.

Yosser
    Oh, the grand old Duke of York,
    He had ten thousand men;
    He marched them up to the top of the hill,
    And he marched them down again.

All
    When they were up, they were up,
    And when they were down, they were down,
    And when they were only halfway up,
    They were neither up nor down!

Around Liverpool.

Others turn up, performing their daily routine/sequence of looking for work.

Chrissie *and* **Loggo**. **Kevin** *and* **Dixie**.

Loggo   Anything goin' here, pal?

Dixie   Yeah I was in last week? You said to come back.

Chrissie   Nothin' doing, I'm guessing?

Loggo   Right.

Chrissie   Awh well.

Kevin   Ta anyway.

Yosser *is following a* **Groundskeeper**.

Yosser   Giz a job. Go on, giz it. I could do that. I could draw lines on a field, straight lines, dead straight they'd be, that's me, dead straight, I could do that, go on giz it, giz a job.

Then he follows a **Milkman**.

Yosser   Oy, giz that job, giz it, go on. I can carry milk. I can get up early. I can milk a cow. I can carry bottles. I can leave things at people's doors, go on. Go on. Go on. Ah go on. Go on. Giz it. Giz it.

The he stops next to a **Lollipop Lady**.

Yosser   Oy giz a job. I could stop traffic, I can hold a lollipop, I won't lick it, I won't, I promise, I won't, go on I could do that. I could do that. Ah giz a job.

The others return.

Loggo   Look I'm sorry to ask.

Chrissie   Yeah I'm sorry to bother, but –

Dixie   Come on, there must be something goin'?

Loggo   Anything?

Kevin   Da-ad?

Dixie   What?!

Loggo   Cheers, then.

Chrissie   Yeah, see ya.

Kevin   Ta'ra.

Dixie   That's your problem, you: you take no for an answer.

Kevin   No *is* the only answer. I've only heard no since I left bleeding school, to every question I've ever asked!

All   No!

They all part, and we find:

Liverpool Metropolitan Cathedral, 'Paddy's Wigwam'.

Yosser *sat in confession, with a* **Catholic Priest**.

Catholic Priest   Yes . . . Hello?

Yosser   . . .

Catholic Priest   Would you like to begin your confession?

It's alright. It's just me and you.

Yosser   And me children.

Catholic Priest   Children? Are there children through there? I shouldn't really hear it in the presence of . . . it's meant to be private. But I suppose if, if it's not a confession of any – consequence.

Yosser *starts to gently sob, trying not to.*

Catholic Priest   Do you want to just talk to me? Just . . . talk? Whatever you want. It's why I'm here.

Yosser   . . . Father?

Catholic Priest   Yes?

Yosser   I'm Yosser Hughes.

Catholic Priest   You don't need to tell me your name. In fact it's –

Yosser   I'm desperate, Father.

Catholic Priest   I see.

Well, look, you've given me your name, Yosser. Why don't I give you mine. Don't call me Father, call me Dan. I'm Dan.

Yosser   I'm desperate, Dan.

Catholic Priest   Go on. Whatever you want to tell me, you can tell me. Through me, you talk to God. He's listening.

Yosser   I thought you said it was private!

Catholic Priest   Well, it, it is, but . . . God is everywhere.

Yosser   You mean he's been here this whole time? Just observin'? Like it's some spectator sport, all this?

Catholic Priest   Well –

Yosser   I need him to take the ball, Father! Get in the friggin' game!

Catholic Priest   Yes but remember . . . as a child of Christ, you do have free will.

Yosser   Free will?

Catholic Priest   Catholicism . . . we believe that you are, to an extent, responsible for your own choices.

Yosser   Pfffff! 'Free will'. Like 'free Markets', then, is it? Those built to thrive, survive, those that weren't, sod 'em?

Catholic Priest   Well –

Yosser   I knew it. God's a Tory.

Catholic Priest   He's what?

Yosser   He's leaving us here to rot.

Catholic Priest   I think . . . if you're after more for that kind of thing . . . you'd have more luck down the road.

Yosser   Down the road?

Catholic Priest   C of E.

Yosser   But they're your competition.

Catholic Priest   Free market. Like you say.

The others re-emerge, like a murmuration of birds.

All   Anything going, mate?

Is there anything doing?

You got anything going, pal?

Nothing at all?

Loggo *remains – staring out – increasingly impassioned and enraged as he goes . . .*

Loggo   I wanna work. Can't you see, I *want* – to work?! You're telling me to get a job, and then you're saying there are none! So what do you want me to do? EY?! What?! I wanta work! I WANTA WORK!

We find:

Liverpool Cathedral.

Yosser *and a* **Protestant Reverend**.

Protestant Reverend   Hello . . .? Yes?

Yosser   Don't mind me, I'm only browsing.

Protestant Reverend   Browsi – . . .? For anything in particular?

Yosser   Salvation. I need to be saved. Ey, do you have any offers on?

This is less nice than the one up the road, no offence or anything.

Protestant Reverend   Ah. Well.

Yosser   Do you know Graeme Sounness?

Protestant Reverend   Graeme Sounness.

Yosser   He stole my look. Magnum too, the pair of them.

I'm Yosser Hughes.

(*Begins sobbing again*.) . . . They've just left us, haven't they? They've left us.

Protestant Reverend   . . . Who?

Yosser (*looking up*)   Him. (*Then.*) *Her*! (*Then.*) Them . . .

I can't sleep. But I keep having this dream. So it can't be a dream, can it. You can't dream if you can't sleep, can yer; maybe it's a vision. Could it be a vision, Father?

Protestant Reverend   Reverend.

Yosser   Could it be a vision, Reverend? Like Moses? Ey, he was on the dole when he had his vision, wasn't he? He'd been kicked out of work?

Protestant Reverend   What's your dream?

Yosser   I'm *falling* . . .

Protestant Reverend   . . . I see. Well. We are the Church of the Risen.

Yosser   So it's possible then? To stop falling? To come back, from the dead? And to rise?

Protestant Reverend   There is certainly precedence, yes.

Yosser (*a moment. Then*)   How do we rise, Father . . .? How do we rise?

Protestant Reverend   We must reach out. And we must believe. And remember that a better place exists, beyond here.

Yosser   Preston?

Protestant Reverend   No, I –

Yosser   The Wirral?

Protestant Reverend   No, I mean –

Yosser   Not Middlesbrough?!

Protestant Reverend   I meant Heaven. Heaven.

Yosser   . . . When I was little. When I was. There was *so much* to look forward to. When I was little . . . I built sandcastles . . .

I thought I knew where I was going once. I did. But there's nowhere left to go.

I know it's my fault. I know I'm to blame, I know that much. But what I want to know is . . . is this all there is? Down to this? Ey? Unless you're somebody. I bet that's shit an'all. I bet Graeme Souness is really unhappy.

Then, a new idea. At the **Protestant Reverend**.

Yosser   Reverend. Giz a job.

Protestant Reverend   Sorry?

Yosser   Yeah I could do that, what you're doing, I can do that, yeah giz it.

Scene Three

Chrissie's backyard.

Chrissie *polishing his gun, and talking to his birds.*

Chrissie   You heard all that, I'm guessing? Me and her, goin' at it?

Yeah well, it's your fault. I shouldn't have given you that bread. The last three slices.

I know that. But they *were* stale. You don't mind stale, do yer.

How much guilt can I take, ey? Where do you go from bread? Bread winner? That's what she's really saying, isn't it. I'm the bread *winner*, or meant to be. The provider.

'That Chrissie Todd. He's too nice, him. Never rocks the boat' . . .

I just don't know what to do.

Polishes his gun.

'Shoddy renovation'. I keep thinking about that. I thought he mainly talked shite, Snowy Malone. But he was right. The foundations are fine. It's what we've done to it since. How careless we were . . .

(*Looking at his gun.*) What am I gonna do, ey? Become a highwayman? The Scouser Pimpernel.

He points the gun, aiming it, pretending to shoot into the air . . .

Loggo *enters, and makes him jump.*

Chrissie   Jesus, I could have taken your bloody head off there, Loggo.

Loggo   Or your own.

Wait that's . . . that's not what yer were –?

Chrissie   What? Oh give over.

(*Puts the gun away.*) What are you doin' here. What's with the bag.

Loggo   I'm going, Chrissie. I'm sorry.

Chrissie *thinks about arguing with him, but realises there's no point.*

Chrissie   Ok.

Loggo   The ship's taking on water, and they expect us to stay on board and hope for the best. Well, I won't.

Chrissie   I understand, Loggo. Who knows, if I was a younger man, if I didn't have a wife, a kid, a home, I'd probably . . .

Loggo (*dumps his bag*)   Ah maybe I'm wrong. Maybe I'm an idiot. It has been known. I'm not even sure where I'll go or if there'll be anything for me when I get there, but . . .

Chrissie   Put it this way, Loggo. What will you miss?

Loggo (*thinks*)   Some things. Not others. The *stories*, Chrissie. I know I shouldn't have gone off at George that time. 'Dockers are storytellers', I know that, but it's always the same old stories. From the same old people. Where are the new stories. Where's *my* story? People like me?

George always says this city exists right on the edge, on the 'outside'. And it's outsiders that they treat us like, and we're outsiders how we live.

Sometimes though. When you even feel on the outside of the outside. D'you know how that can make you feel?

Chrissie   Inside out?

Loggo (*smiles*)   Yeah.

Chrissie *offers his hand.* **Loggo** *takes it.*

Chrissie   Goodbye, Loggo.

Loggo   Goodbye, Chrissie.

He goes.

Chrissie *enters his house.*

Inside.

Angie *facing away from* **Chrissie**.

Chrissie   Is this the silent treatment?

Ok, good, that's cleared that up, then.

The main problem with the silent treatment, of course, is that its ineffectiveness as a weapon of war stems from the fact that the victim is unable to ascertain what exactly he's done to bleedin' merit it.

Angie   What's the point, gas has gone, can't cook anything anyway if there were anything in the fridge, which there isn't. Until they come and cut that off.

Chrissie (*had enough, pacing away*)   Yeah until they cut that off, and then there'll be nothing left *to* cut off. Except me!

Angie   I can't cut off what you haven't got!

Chrissie   You know, I didn't think you could hurt me anymore. But there again. Practice makes perfect.

Angie   You've been offered a way out, and you won't take it.

Chrissie   Take what? That job from Malloy, is that what you want?

Angie   It isn't about 'want'. 'Want' is for other people.

Chrissie   I can't do it. It isn't right.

Angie   Do you think the others wouldn't?

Chrissie   I can't speak for them, can I? I can only speak for myself.

Angie   You could pick up the phone, right now. Phone him. Phone Malloy.

Chrissie   You don't get it.

Angie   I don't get it!

Chrissie   It's the principle.

Angie   Oh yeah. I remember them.

Chrissie   Angie . . .

Angie   You've been given a chance to *do* something. You've got to *do* something!

Chrissie   I am doing something! I'm going to court! And then I'm going to get a very heavy fine which I will not be able to pay. And then I'm going to go to jail! And you?! You can go and live with your mother. An event you've been looking forward to for a long time.

Angie   God, you don't know anything about me, do yer, you don't know me.

Chrissie   That's right, I have this amazing gift to live with someone in the same house for eleven years and not know who they are.

I don't know what love is either, do I? Well, it obviously isn't an empty fridge and the gas cut off, is it?

Angie   Oh go and tell it to your chickens! Ruffle *their* feathers instead.

Chrissie   And when we get evicted. When we're standing there on the street well and truly finished with each other if that's what love's about.

She finds herself hitting his chest and he grabs her to stop.

Chrissie   Oh yeah. You as well, ey? Yeah well go on then, one free shot.

She does, breaking free and they fall back on top of one another on the sofa, as she hits him and weeps.

Angie   Yeah why not, why not, why not . . . for God's sake, for once in your life, why don't you stand up for yourself?! Fight back . . . (*Giving up, exhausted.*) . . . fight *back* . . .

He doesn't fight back, eventually breaking and collapsing into a curled-up ball.

They break. Catching their breath . . .

Chrissie   I had a job. It wasn't a bad job and I was good at it.

I laid the roads, girl, I laid the roads.

Motorways, lay-bys, country lanes.

I could temper and grit like nobody you ever saw. Nobody could put down the blackstuff like me. And it's alright, I deserved to lose it. I betrayed them.

Angie   Who? Dixie?

Chrissie   Yes. And no. All of them. Something bigger. By just looking out for myself. And I won't do it again.

Angie (*picking up the phone*)   Phone him. Take the job.

Chrissie   . . . George, the others –

Angie   They'll understand!

Chrissie   This can't be it! That that's all it is, now. Dog eat dog.

Angie   You find me a dog, I'll bloody eat it! Because I am *hungry*, Chrissie.

Chrissie   It's not my fault you know, it's not my fault!

Angie   And it's not mine. But at least you have a *choice*.

. . . I am twenty-eight years old, Chrissie.

Chrissie   What's that got to do – . . .

Angie   I am twenty-eight years old. I married you when I was seventeen, I was a mother at eighteen –

Chrissie *gets back out of the bed, growling. Getting changed again.*

Angie   – and I'm not blaming you for that, it takes two to tango.

But I'm a person, and I live, and breathe, and fart after five lagers and lime and I have a mind up here and it is screaming. It can't take much more.

I've never had a life outside of you and Justine and Clare. That's all.

I was going to, I was going to do a lot, be out in the world, 'Hi. Angie.' This was going to be my time. And what's happened since? What have I got? Half a tin of spam and hole in my left shoe.

Chrissie   Well, just walk on one leg then, you'll be alright –

She throws some keys at him.

Angie   It is not funny. It is not friggin' funny. I've had a enough of that 'if you don't laugh you'll cry'. I've heard it for years, this stupid sodding city is full of it! Why *don't* you cry? Why don't you scream, why don't you fight back, you bastard, why don't you fight back, Chrissie Todd! Because if you haven't had enough of it I have.

Chrissie*'s almost had enough. He marches over to the phone.*

Picks up the receiver, hovering in the air . . .

He's almost shaking . . .

He can't do it, slamming it back down and sits on the floor.

Chrissie   . . . What do you think it's like. For me. Ey? A second-class citizen. A second-rate man. With no money and no job and no . . . no . . . nooo – *place*!

Angie (*calmer. Resigned*)   Tell it to me kids, Chrissie. Tell it to the cupboards and fridge. See how full your words can make them. And when you do, you make breakfast, and then you'll have finally found a job. You'll have become a frigging magician.

Chrissie *boils over, and stands.*

Chrissie   Yeah . . . I'll fill 'em. You see if I don't. And I hope you sodding enjoy it!

He heads at pace . . .

. . . into Chrissie's backyard.

He loads his shotgun, and fires.

Just as **Angie** *comes out of the door in her dressing gown.*

Bird feathers seem to fall about him, from above, like snow . . .

He weeps, tossing the gun down and falling to his knees.

Angie *joins him.*

Holding him. Nothing else to do . . .

Scene Four

To Dixie's house.

Kevin*'s bedroom.*

Kevin *is playing his guitar.*

Dixie *watches him, unseen for a moment. Before –*

Dixie   Sounds good.

Kevin   Ta.

Silence.

You been out?

Dixie   Yeah. (*Then.*) Out me mind.

Kevin   I'll get dressed in a minute, I will –

Dixie   Why bother?

(*Off his look.*) You're right. You were right.

Kevin   I might just go out tonight then.

Dixie   What am I going to do?

Kevin   You mean tonight?

Dixie   No I don't mean tonight.

Kevin *watches his dad. Suddenly worried.*

Kevin   I'll make the rounds tomorrow, Dad. I promise. You never know –

Dixie   Do you *want* a job?

Kevin *doesn't answer.* **Dixie** *paces the room, hands in pocket, or leans against the door, not quite knowing how to do this . . .*

Dixie   What if you was to leave home?

This sits in the room.

Kevin   Are you asking me if I want to?

Or . . . like, do yo – . . .

Dixie   Would yer? Would you leave home?

Kevin *nods.*

Dixie   None of us are helping each other.

Fighting never seems to lead nowhere except another fight.

There's no jobs in this town, there's not many jobs in every other town, but there's more jobs out of town than this town.

Long contracts, you can get.

He looks at his son.

I know it isn't what you want, but what I'm doing isn't what I want either.

Kevin   You don't have to tell me. I know that.

I know that, Dad. I know.

Dixie *nods, and begins to leave. Stopping. He speaks this very carefully . . .*

Dixie   If I'd any sense . . . if I'd known what was going to happen. I wouldn't have done some of the things I have done. To you.

I sort of . . . I made a lot of mistakes. With you. Son.

He leaves the room. Without looking back.

The street.

Yosser *is fronting up to a* **Debt Collector** *outside.*

Debt Collector   I don't think you understand, Mr Hughes, I'm a bailiff –

Yosser   Not now, not now!

Debt Collector   I'm the nice one they send before the thugs and brutes get sent in, and –

Yosser   Not now! Not while me kids are with me –

(*Pointing at them, inside.*) Look at 'em, pride and joy, these three. Maurice here – Maurice, stop pickin' y' nose! He's a natural, he is. Natural. Tranmere Rovers have sent scouts already to see him, and he's only seven, oh yeah.

Debt Collector (*confused*)   Mr Hughes . . .

Yosser   And look at these two, Dustin and Ann-Marie. They'll grow out of them knocked knees, you watch. The brand new Torvill and Dean! I'm tellin' yer –

Debt Collector   Are you having me on, pal? This crap about your 'kids' –

Yosser (*turning on him*)   You and me would look good outside, pal . . .

Debt Collector (*nervous*)   . . . We are outside.

Yosser *headbutts him. And steps over him.*

Yosser   Come on, kids . . . Can't say I didn't warn him.

Back at **Chrissie***'s house.*

George *arrives. He's now having to use a walker, which he walks as he wheels.*

George   Hello?

Angie   Uncle George . . .? Here, come in.

George   I'm alright, Ang, I'm ok.

Chrissie   George. What are you doing here?

George   You never come to me. Why are you the only one, Chrissie, who never comes to me? When you're the only one I reckon I can actually *help*.

Chrissie   Help with what? The dole? Don't worry about that, you're sick.

George   If I'm treated like a sick man, I will be a sick man.

Chrissie   Come on. I'm taking you back.

George (*quietly, producing a fiver*)   Ey. Look. See? Let's go for a drink.

Chrissie   In *your* state –

At that point – the old walker breaks, falling to bits.

Angie/Chrissie   Oh, Christ/What the bleedin' . . .?

George   Aggh. Falling to pieces. Like everything else.

Please, Chrissie. One last one for the road . . .

Chrissie   George, you can barely friggin' stand.

George   I've got me wheelchair, at home.

Chrissie (*to* **Angie**)   Can I?

(*She nods.*) I'll go get it, wait here.

Chrissie *heads off at speed.*

George   Ey . . .

He takes her hand and gives her some money.

George   Here.

Angie   No, *no*, George, I can't, I –

He closes her hand around the money.

George   It's ok. You're ok . . .

Angie *doesn't know what to say, and almost bursts into tears.*

She rests his head on his shoulder . . .

And then – some noise, out in the street . . .

To **Yosser**'s *house.*

Banging on the door. **Yosser** *inside.*

Policeman   Mr Hughes! Mr Hughes! You've been given your notice, it's time!

Yosser *faces away. Not moving.*

Policeman   Mr Hughes, open the door, this is the police. Just come to the door, Mr Hughes.

Outside – **Chrissie** *arrives with* **George***.*

Chrissie   Ey, ey, what's going on with Yosser?

Policeman   You know this arsehole? He assaulted a bailiff and then locked the door. Mr Hughes?!

Dixie *arrives from his house, too.*

Dixie   Chrissie?

Chrissie   I think he's finally tipped over the edge, Dix.

Policeman   Right. Stand back from the door!

The door gets kicked in. The **Policeman** *raises his baton –*

We're coming in, don't be a silly bugger, right?

Chrissie   No, no look, let *us* have a word, ok, there's no need for all that. You'll only make it all worse.

Policeman   . . . Two minutes.

Chrissie   George?

George (*too weak*)   You go. You take this one, Chrissie.

Chrissie *and* **Dixie** *head inside.*

Yosser *doesn't look around, just faces away, back turned.*

Chrissie   Yosser?

Yosser   . . . Yeah. That's me. I'm Yosser Hughes. This is my house. I don't want them in my house.

Dixie   Yosser. No good can come of this, friend, ok? –

Yosser   'Friend'?

Dixie   . . . Yeah, Yosser. Friend. Why not?

Yosser   It was that shrink, wasn't it. She wrote her report, didn't she?

I could do that, I could be a shrink. I could work people out. You know why they call them shrinks, right. Because they shrink people. Well, not me. Because I'm Yosser Hughes. She tried that. She used to shrink everything. One wash, fit for a dwarf.

They're not taking my kids. They are not taking them –

Chrissie   Yosser, for Christ's sake, stop it. Your kids – . . . your kids are *gone*.

Yosser *doesn't say anything*.

Chrissie   They've been gone for *months*, mate, you know that. After she left yer.

Dixie   They took 'em off yer, Yoss. You– . . . you tried you best, but this pretending. It has to stop.

Chrissie   On the building site? In the dole? The poached eggs, for Christ's sake!

We can see, you know, mate. We can see they're not there. It has to stop . . .

Yosser *lowers his head*.

Chrissie   . . . I know that must be – . . . actually I don't know. I don't know that 'must be' anything. But I do know some things. I know this is only going to end in tears, if you don't just come out of here without trouble, ok.

Yosser   . . . You're too nice, Chrissie Todd. Always been too nice.

Policeman   Alright, enough chat –

Chrissie   No –

They're shoved out the way by the **Policeman**.

Yosser *starts swinging, screaming, kicking, swinging his fists violently.*

The rest of the room fades away.

Just him. Swinging. Kicking. Swinging. Head-butting. Swinging. Kicking. Screaming.

To a roadside.

Loggo, *who arrives by a road, with a hitchhiker's sign.*

Further down the road is **Kevin**.

They see and acknowledge each other.

Loggo *turns his sign around to show* **Kevin**. *'Shetlands'.*

Kevin *shows* **Loggo** *his sign. 'Leeds'.*

They both smile . . .

To the docks.

Chrissie *arrives, wheeling* **George** *in his wheelchair. Incredibly frail.*

Chrissie   Alright, ace. Look at these hot wheels, ey?

George   Liverpool docks, ey, son. Saturday dinner time. And not a soul about.

Once upon a time, Chrissie.

Chrissie   If you're going to tell me about Cinderella.

George   We'd be looking forward to it from the previous Saturday.

Pay day, Saturday, you know

Ah there'd be hundreds of us coming along here. The ship repair men, scalers, dockers. The Mary Ellens who used to swab the big liners.

And behind them the great big shire cart horses.

Ah, Chrissie, there were many a good horse walked down that hill, but they're come back up in a knacker's cart.

And yet. The horses of 'privilege', that pose outside Buckingham Palace and ponce and parade up and down the Mall? Turned out into a meadow. Full of cowslip and clover. A full proven bag, for the rest of their lives . . .

(*Sighs*.) Ah, Chrissie . . . it just seems like yesterday, the midday gun. Listen . . .

They listen out for it. It doesn't come.

The women sandstoning the steps and the flags.

The kids playing alley-oh, the little shops on the corner where you got the three pennyworth of fine Irish, the old snuff, the twist of tobacco, and your old gran had a flat-top cart there, *there*, used to sell salt fish and a big barrel of ribs, straight off the pig's back from the Irish boat . . .

And there we'd be pilin' into Effin Nellie's, or Peg-Leg Pete's for a couple of pints of good beer, maybe the first in the week and the crack. The crack! We'd talk of many things.

Chrissie   Of cabbages and kings.

George   Of politics and power and come the day when we'd have inside toilets and proper bathrooms. Of Attlee, and Bevan, Hogan and Logan, the Braddocks and Dixie Dean . . . and Lawton and Liddell and Matthews and Finney . . . Of come the revolution, and the Blackpool illuminations. And Joey Jones had a violin, a 'Stradavarious', he said . . .

Well. We've got our bathrooms. At considerable expense . . .

He struggles to catch his breath. Weakening.

George   Get me up, son. Let me stand up.

Chrissie   Are you sure, George?

He helps him stand. **George** *grabbing on to* **Chrissie** *now. Almost shaking him . . . because he's struggling? Or because he's really shaking him now, shaking him out of it . . .*

George   Why can't they stand up, Chrissie? As a – 'people' . . . Why don't you stand up, Chrissie Todd –

Chrissie (*struggling*)   George –

George   Fight back. Fight back . . .

Chrissie   . . .

George *looks out across the docks.*

George   Forty-seven years ago, I stood here. A young bull. And watched my first ship come in . . .

They say memories live longer than dreams. But my dreams, those dreams, those dreams of long ago, they still give me some kind of hope. And faith, in my class. I can't believe there's no hope. I *can't* . . .

Chrissie *helps him back down into his seat.*

Chrissie   Alright, George. It's time. Pints will be on the bar, Loggo and . . .

He looks at **George***, who is almost completely still.*

Chrissie   George?

Tries to stir him, gently.

Pints on the bar, George . . .

He knows he's dead. **Chrissie** *turns, and looks back out across the water.*

Scene Five

All of the **Boys** *return, in their line, putting on their suits as they did for* **Snowy***.*

All (*singing*)
. . . Get some sail upon her
Haul away your halyards
Haul away your halyards
It's our sailing time.

*Here they exist simultaneously in the Department of Employment
and the Liverpool Metropolitan Cathedral.*

Voice of Clerk   Name.

Chrissie   Chrissie Todd.

Dixie   Dixie Dean.

And . . . where **George** *would normally be.*

Catholic Priest   Patrick Malone, oh Lord.

Chrissie (*looks*; *to himself*)   George . . .

Catholic Priest   Show your mercy to this dear departed
servant. Since he strove to do your will, let he not be
punished for wrongdoing.

Voice of Clerk   Have you been employed in any capa –

Catholic Priest   My brothers and sisters, to prepare
ourselves to celebrate the sacred mysteries, let us call to
mind our sins. Rejoice, and be glad for your reward . . .

Voices of All Clerks   Your full entitled benefits . . .

Chrissie/Dixie/Angie/Mrs Malone   Praise to you, Lord
Jesus Christ.

Catholic Priest   I am sure the family and friends of Patrick
Malone –

Chrissie (*publicly, now*)   *George* Malone.

Sorry, Margaret, but I'm right aren't I? See? He was George
Malone.

Yosser   I'm Yosser Hughes.

Catholic Priest   Forgive me. But he was christened, here, as Patrick, and that is his name as known to Almighty God –

Angie   Yeah, well, it don't matter what his name was known under by Almighty God, means nothing to the people here.

She looks to **Chrissie***, who typically says nothing.*

Dixie   Yeah, and by the way, if you don't mind me asking, is Almighty God still employed in any capacity? Is he still residing at his known address, only a lot of us here haven't heard from him for a while.

Catholic Priest   It's clear how well loved . . . 'George' was. I've never seen the congregation so full. Let us remember that we are *all* children of the Almighty. And if we die, we die for the Lord. We shall have to stand before the judgement seat of God, as scripture says: Be my life, it is the Lord who speaks, every knee shall bend before me, and every tongue shall praise God. It is to God, therefore, that each of us must give an account –

Chrissie (*standing now, louder*)   I'm sorry, Father. I am. But you're not on.

Everyone looks.

We haven't come here to listen to this. I don't mean to tell you how to do your job. You're – . . . you're the only one here who's got a job. But you'd better know. We're all here today not to send George to a . . . a 'better place'. Wherever that is. Or to worry about our own going. But to remember his life, and curse the fact that he's not here.

He was a good man. He was the best man I ever knew. I . . .

. . . I loved George Malone. And our lives are going to be a lot emptier now he's not here. He didn't do nothing for no 'rewards'. Or for no Judgment Day. Not here. Nor in Heaven.

In the Department of Employment.

Voice of Clerk   Mr Todd? Miss Sutcliffe would like to see you.

Dixie (*at* **Chrissie**)   What's all that about?

Chrissie   Judgment Day.

Miss Sutcliffe's *office*. **Moss** *present*. **Chrissie** *waiting*.

Miss Sutcliffe   Mr Todd. Christopher Robin Todd.

Chrissie   Ay, that's me. Get it over with.

Miss Sutcliffe   As you know, we have been conducting our investigation into the events of that day, with our very best men, isn't that right, Mr Moss?

Moss   That's right.

Miss Sutcliffe   And we have reached the following conclusion. I do not intend to let the case regarding you gentlemen from Liverpool 8 to go forward.

Chrissie   You what?

Moss   You *what*?! But –

Miss Sutcliffe   A man was killed –

Chrissie   He has a name. Snowy Malone.

Miss Sutcliffe   Snowy Malone was killed because he tried to escape. From us. And though we are authorised to 'chase' you . . . the regrettable nature of this situation calls for some leniency, I think.

Moss   Miss Sutcliffe, shouldn't we –

Chrissie   You're letting me off?

Miss Sutcliffe   All of you. You, Loggo Logmond, Yosser Hughes and George Malone.

Chrissie (*looks around him*)   Looks like I'm the last man standing, doesn't it.

Miss Sutcliffe   It's my understanding that Mr Malloy had 'intended' to put you all on permanent salaries. Therefore I have recommended the contract be returned to his company and you get back to work immediately.

You've got a job, Mr Todd.

Chrissie *doesn't know what to say.*

He's about to get mad, fists clenched . . . but then he doesn't. He might burst into tears instead.

But he doesn't. He shakes his head, and leaves.

Moss   What the bloody hell is all that? We have the evidence? This could have been good for us, upstairs.

Miss Sutcliffe   Upstairs?

Moss   The metaphorical upstairs. Down south. Powers that be –

Miss Sutcliffe   You once asked what I made of you, Donald, remember. The fact is that I like you. I like you . . . because you don't catch people. Because you aren't very good.

Moss   . . . ey?!

You . . . you *don't* want to catch them? (*Realising.*) You don't want to catch them, do you?

Miss Sutcliffe (*spraying her plants, deflecting*)   Who?

Moss   Them! The fraudsters. The cheats. The bad guys.

Miss Sutcliffe   Oh, I want to catch them, Donald. I want to catch *them*. Very much indeed.

Moss   I, I, I . . . (*Laughs, tragically.*) . . . I don't know what to say, the whole thing is absurd. I don't think I can bear it, I think I'm going mad. It's like this whole city is teetering on a knife edge, about to, to, to *snap*.

Miss Sutcliffe   Calm down, Donald. Have a cup of tea.

Moss   I think I'd rather be out there, with them! At least there's something honest about their dishonesty.

Miss Sutcliffe   You must do what you must do, Donald. It is only us doing our job, on this side of the line, that prevents us from being out there, lining up with them, after all. None of it makes sense. None of it is meant to. Madness is the point.

(*Closing the file on the* **Boys**.) And we all deal with it in our own little way.

She exits, leaving him alone.

He turns, as though newly joining a queue, as the lights fade in on him.

Voice of Clerk   Name?

Moss   Donald Moss.

Voice   Are you employed in any capacity?

Moss   . . . No, I am not . . .

Malloy's building site.

Chrissie *is laying the blackstuff when* **Malloy** *joins.*

Malloy   Alright, Chrissie? It's good to be back, isn't it? Where are the others?

Chrissie   A better place? I dunno.

Malloy   Look, I – I am sorry about . . . look it's a war, isn't it? Everyone for themselves –

Chrissie   I don't need any talk, Mr Malloy. I just want to work.

Malloy   And it's work you can be proud of, see? Didn't your boys want to know what new premises it was we were building here?

Chrissie   I couldn't give a toss –

Some tarpaulin is pulled down to reveal the new sign for the building.

The new Department for Employment branch.

Chrissie *doesn't know what to say at first.*

Chrissie   You are fucking joking.

Malloy   And there's more where that came from. They're expanding all the time. Good for you and me, Chrissie. Good for us.

Chrissie *starts laughing to himself. Harder and harder.*

Malloy   What? What is it, Chrissie? What's so funny?

Chrissie   Somewhere in there, frozen for all time. A dedication, whether they like it or not.

'Snowy Malone. 1982.'

He is left alone, laughing.

And maybe they'll never know, but I always will! We will. Even if it all crumbles and turns to dust, in time. What he stood for, and you George . . . (*Looking up.*) . . . and all of 'em. That has to stand the test of time. It has to.

Well, it fucking well better had. Somehow . . .

'Laying the roads, lah. Just laying the roads . . .'

As he lays down the blackstuff, singing quietly to himself.

Oh you can talk about the concrete,
And the boys who work the train
And the fellas in the hopper in the sun and wind and rain,
But the boys who work the blackstuff, sure they're really rough and tough . . .

Yosser *arrives on the site. Watching* **Chrissie** *work.*

Chrissie *stops once he clocks him.*

Yosser *approaches . . . What's he going to do now?*

Yosser   . . . Are you still 'nice'? Chrissie Todd?

A moment. **Chrissie** *might nod uncertainly.*

A brief reconnection, between old friends perhaps. Until –

Yosser   Ey, I can do that!

Snap to black.

Curtain.